Foo... and the Stones of Time

**Dr. Carl Baugh
and
Dr. Clifford Wilson**
with David Ingraham

All scripture references are from the King James Version unless otherwise stated.

FOOTPRINTS AND THE STONES OF TIME
Copyright © 1992 by Dr. Carl Baugh
Glen Rose, Texas

Printed in the United States of America

Published by:
Hearthstone Publishing
901 N.W. 6th Street
Oklahoma City, OK 73106
(405) 235-5396 ● WATS 1-800-652-1144
FAX (405) 236-4634

ISBN 1-879366-17-7

Table of Contents

The Paluxy River is beautiful...
until flash floods temporarily
destroy that beauty, and rip up its
limestone ledges.

Introduction

This started as an edited version of a dialogue between Dr. Carl Baugh and Dr. Clifford Wilson. A series of talks was presented over the radio network of Southwest Radio Church in Oklahoma City with Pastor David Ingraham as the very capable host who kept two enthusiastic scholars tied to the fascinating subjects they were dealing with.

After the programs had been presented, each of the participants felt that there were areas needing elaboration, and these are dealt with in Part III.

But there's an old saying, ''A picture is worth a thousand words.'' So Dr. Wilson accepted the pleasant responsibility of bringing together a series of pictures which would be of interest as well as being convincing evidence to clench the arguments already developed in this book. These are presented in Part II.

Three specialized areas are dealt with...Footprints, Stones, and Time--as far as possible in layman's language. May you be blessed as you read, and may Jesus Christ be glorified.

--Dr. Carl Baugh

Part I

Facing the Issues

Chapter One
Let's Talk About Evolution and Creation

Dr. Wilson: The title of this book is *Footprints and the Stones of Time*, and the ramifications of the title are threefold. We are thinking in terms of three major concepts: first, the concept of footprints--"footprints *in* the stones of time" if you like. But we are not only thinking of footprints, for there are two other aspects as well, hence the title *Footprints and the Stones of Time*. We will especially deal with footprints such as those at the Paluxy River in Texas.

Then there are stones, such as limestone ledges, and also there are writings in stones and on clay tablets. So we will also be talking about stones with writing on them--archaeological artifacts.

Dr. Baugh: We know about actual human footprints on an international scale. Some have been found in Australia; some have been found near Moab in Utah. We have academically documented extensive trails of human footprints in Glen Rose, Texas. We will even talk about Turkey--I have just returned from an extensive visit to that country and they have found two human footprints, moderately large in size, and the stunning thing about this is that these are found in Cretaceous context by and large. That means that many individuals--at least those that walked in Australia, those that walked in Utah, and those that walked in Texas--these individuals lived at the time of the dinosaurs . . .

What Is This Cretaceous Stratum?

Dr. Wilson: Hey, Dr. Baugh, just a minute! You have been using a big word; I know what it means, but I am sure many other people don't, even though they are not Australians! What's this word "Cretaceous" you are talking about?

Dr. Baugh: All right! We are just having a "hearthstone" conversation here. In the standard geological terminology, according to the theory of evolution, life began to develop--to evolve seriously--a little over six hundred million years ago . .

Dr. Wilson: Excuse me, my textbook says five hundred million.

Dr. Baugh: Well, it depends on what publication you are reading. Actually, this is a very serious point--the geological ages given are basically speculation; they cannot be substantiated at all!

Dr. Wilson: That is my point. They throw out a hundred million years as though it were a couple of days or weeks.

Dr. Baugh: Yes, and though they do throw dates around, they really are not there. It is conjecture and speculation. Now our Creator has been around forever. He is eternal, but the creation itself is very recent. Jesus said that God made Adam and Eve from the beginning of the creation.

Dr. Wilson: What do you mean by "very recent," Dr. Baugh?

Dr. Baugh: A matter of thousands of years--less than ten thousand, I would say.

Dr. Wilson: Only about twenty years ago I would have said that you were talking nonsense. I don't now.

Dr. Baugh: I think it is fascinating that you are a scholar--in my opinion one of the finest creation scholars on the global scene--and yet, years ago you taught the long-age concept. Decades ago, I personally espoused the concept of evolution, and taught the long-age concept. But I was not aware that Dr. Wilson had earlier accepted that the earth was millions of years old. Then in a book we published together, he admitted in print that a scholar had changed his mind, and he came to see that there is academic evidence--overwhelming evidence--to support recency, by which I mean thousands of years.

Dr. Wilson: As far as I was concerned twenty years ago, the earth could be millions or even billions of years old. I talked about "progressive creation," but it really was close to what some people called "theistic evolution." I've long since come away from that position.

Dr. Baugh: Evolution did not take place at all; it is a religious concept. It actually supports a humanistic outlook which is a religious concept in its primary doctrinal dogma. But let me come back to your question about Cretaceous time. This is the period of time assigned an age of 144 million to 64 million years ago. That means that we are giving reference to a timescale set by evolutionary geology; they set it as if evolution were true, and the bottom line of the evidence is that we have found human prints among dinosaur prints, and that shows conclusively that the geological scale is not a reality at all. Cretaceous time is simply recent time, and all the so-called geological epochs existed simultaneously. They were brought about by a global deluge that we refer to as the worldwide flood.

What's This Theory of Evolution?

Dr. Wilson: May I pick up on a word that you used? You have referred to the theory of evolution. Strictly speaking there is no such thing! As you know, you don't start with a theory, you start with a hypothesis. You observe certain things and say, "This looks like the way it works." If after enough observations it becomes accepted--I do not mean just five, six, seven, but a vast number of observations--it becomes accepted as a theory. Then when the theory is so widely accepted that there is no possibility of refuting it, it becomes known as a law. The fact is, the concept of evolution has never got beyond the hypothesis stage; it is a religious commitment; it is not a true scientific theory.

Dr. Baugh: Do you suggest that somebody has had a vested interested in superimposing the title "theory" over something that is only a hypothesis--and a very poor one at that? How do we explain this kind of thing--why is this being perpetrated?

Dr. Wilson: I'll tell you in one sentence. They do not want to accept the concept of God...because of accountability in such matters as spiritual values. If it was not that there are spiritual overtones in what we are talking about with the Paluxy River footprints, there would be no argument about human and dinosaur footprints being there together. But that means that you come back to recency, to God having spoken just a few thousand years ago and instantaneous creation followed--and so there really is no argument. It brings you back to God, and to the spiritual accountability that follows.

Dr. Baugh: We should be prepared to accept the authority imposed by a Creator, and the Bible is the only defendable written source text about creation in all the world...and what a text it is! It is inerrant, and the integrity of Scripture can be verified academically: there is verification even in the scientific matters we are looking at. We speak about historic footprints, and we give the implications--whether the implication is humanistic or creationistic--we give the implications so that the issues can be considered clearly. Once the footprint is substantiated, what does that do for our accountability? And the credibility of the creation model? The creation model is absolutely credible. One major scholar said recently that the theory of evolution is untenable, totally unprovable, but the alternative is unthinkable.

He was, of course, referring to the alternative of special creation. We know it is *not* unthinkable, but it does involve the necessity to accept the fact of the all-powerful God who created.

Pastor Ingraham: I need to ask this question--by the way, I am already convinced. If I play the Devil's advocate, I am sure that you will understand. If we say that creationism is our model, isn't that inherently a religious concept? How can we present that from an academic point of view?

Dr. Baugh: I lecture across the country at high schools, colleges, and universities, private and public. I lecture on scientific creationism and in strictly academic arenas, and unless the professor or one of the students brings up the biblical record, I stick with the so-called scientific model. I am not ashamed of the Bible in the least, because at the same time I lecture and preach in Christian circles.

The evidence is overwhelming, and it is so documented academically and scientifically that every point of the creation model should be upheld. I refer to such matters as the world that existed before the global deluge, the superiority of life at the time of life's origin, the absolute impossibility of evolutionary progression, the absolute impossibility of an evolutionary origin of life, or of the naturalistic origin of life. The evidence for creation is absolutely overwhelming.

If we simply approach it from an academic standpoint, there is only one tenable position--that is, we were designed and created instantaneously, just a few thousand years ago.

The Evolutionist's Faith

Dr. Wilson: What is more, you have to have much more faith these days, with the knowledge that is available, to believe in evolution than to believe in creation. The Psalmist says, *"The fool hath said in his heart, There is no God . . ."* (Ps. 14:1). Do you know that apart from the red cells, the separate individual cells of our bodies (with certain exceptions) contain billions of pieces of data, interrelated and interdependent? This leads us to the fact that we have no option but to accept the concept of a Great Designer and Creator. It is still true that the fool has said in his heart, "There is no God." That is where we are today.

Dr. Baugh: In fact, all life forms had to be created simultaneously. They are so interdependent and anterially related. Two of the world's leading astrophysicists, Sir Frederick Hoyle, Ph.D., and Dr. Chandra Wickwamasingh, Ph.D., spent over two decades analyzing all the data they had in their computer banks--the best available information on a global scale. They began as atheists, but once they assimilated all the data relating to life and the information about the interrelationship of life, they came to the conclusion that the chance of life originating by chance--not just man and all his complicated relationships, but **life** itself originating by natural processes on Planet Earth--is one in ten to the 40,000th power. They went on to illustrate that by saying that those odds would be less than the probability of a whirlwind sweeping through a junkyard and assembling a Boeing 747 jet in flight at the other end. That flight pattern could be undertaken easier than life originating on Planet Earth by chance.

Dr. Wilson: Yet one of the sad things is that though they came to that conclusion--and therefore in a sense they became creationists--they do not accept the God of the Bible. They came back to such concepts as, ''Go beyond our planet to beings from outer space,'' etc.--almost like Erich Von Daniken and his *Chariots Of the Gods*. I wrote a book years ago called *Crash Go the Chariots*, and many of the things Von Daniken is talking about as coming from outer space are plain nonsensical.

Dr. Baugh: It is really ''passing the buck.'' If life originated somewhere else the chances may have been even greater than we have suggested--that is, with life even less likely. Let me address this for a moment. Dr. Robert Gange is a leading scholar who worked with NASA extensively. Let us take the entire universe as we address this thing of transpermia for a moment. The position of Hoyle and Wickwamasingh is that, while life could not have originated on Planet Earth, perhaps it originated somewhere else in the universe, and was transferred by intelligent beings. Over evolutionary spans of time apparently they had acquired the intelligence to travel and to leave their garbage here, or to manipulate the forces on Planet Earth.

That is a form of creation, even if it is another evolved being that does it. Of course we do not agree with that kind of creationism. Dr. Gange came up with some interesting statistics that have been verified in laboratories on a global scale.

Could Life Have Evolved Somewhere Else?

Let's take all the natural elements on Planet Earth, from uranium back down to hydrogen. Let's presume we have all the information available in the interchange of the atoms and the interchange between atoms and chemical elements. We find that all the information available in all the natural elements on Planet Earth can be expressed in one hundred sixty exponential bits of information. All the information available in the entire solar system can be expressed in one hundred seventy exponential bits of information. For the entire universe it is two hundred thirty-five bits of information--that is the outer limit. We are talking about all the information available in all the natural elements in the entire universe: we are asking ourselves, "Could life have evolved somewhere else? And could it have been brought here to Planet Earth from another planet?"

If the universe is as big as Dr. Carl Sagan wants it to be (it is as big as the Creator wants it to be), by any stretch of the imagination the largest estimate would be two hundred thirty-five exponential bits of information throughout the entire universe. In contradistinction, when we come to life, the smallest unit of life we know anything about is a protein molecule. A protein molecule cannot even replicate itself. It has to have a host cell to produce it, but it is a living thing. That is the smallest unit of living material that we know anything about.

The information in one protein molecule is fifteen hundred exponential bytes of information. But wait a minute: the natural elements of the earth and the natural elements of the entire universe only have two hundred thirty-five exponential bits of information available, but the exponential bits in one tiny molecule are so interrelated, it has fifteen hundred exponential bits. Let's take that a step further. *E. Coli* bacteria in our digestive tracts hold seven million exponential bits and one human cell holds twenty billion exponential bits of information!

The Most Scientific Statement Ever Made!

Just what does that matter? The bottom line is: Give the universe its primordial pool, and put a pool on every planet. Better still: put one on every acre of every planet. Better still: take every planet, every star optimal in temperature, lightning strokes, available energy, and make the entire universal structure a primordial pool of soup, with just the right elements. Give it not sixteen billion years of time that the evolutionists want...give it an eternity of time. Scientifically, if every element and every bit of information on that element had time to writhe and contort with every other element throughout the entire universe, there is not enough information available, given that eternity of time, to produce one living unit of matter. The most scientific statement I have ever read is in Genesis 1:1, *"In the beginning God created...."*

Dr. Wilson: Isn't it beautiful? "In the beginning"--that is how the Genesis record is introduced. I find, among other things, it is tremendously interesting when you come to Genesis 1, there is not the so-called cosmological argument discussed, nor the ontological argument, nor the teleological argument, nor any of the other usual philosophical arguments about the existence of God. We are simply brought to the fact, *"In the beginning God created...."* It is a self-evident fact that there is a God, and the scriptural approach is, *"...he that cometh to God must believe that he is, and that he is a rewarder of them that diligently seek him"* (Heb. 11:6). Faith is demanded! The evolutionist who listens to all that highly relevant material that you have just given has no way of getting past it. Academically, scientifically, methodologically, he has no way of getting past it. Any investigator of integrity is forced to acknowledge that there is intelligence behind it all, and that something is not something--it is Someone. As Genesis 1:1 puts it, "Bara Elohim!"--"God created"--or if you like to use the English order of words, "Elohim bara."

Let me give you a little spiritual point about that "Bara Elohim"--in the first verse of the Bible, *Elohim* is the Hebrew masculine plural for "God," and *bara* is the singular form of the verb "to create." So the verse is saying, "The Gods, He created." It is not actually saying "the Trinity," but I suggest it is implicit. Over and over again in the Old Testament you have beautiful teaching that is implicit, and then later it is made explicit: it is brought out into the open in the New Testament. So in the New Testament we have the Trinity: the Father, the Son, and the Holy Spirit--each member of the Trinity is identified as being there at creation. We accept that by faith, but it is beautiful in reality. God created us, and the God who created us is the same God who sent His Son to die on the cross to give us forgiveness of sins.

Dr. Baugh: It would be a great tragedy for anyone to agree with all this information, and yet not to accept the Creator Himself. Each of us can know Him in the Person of His Son-- in fact, that is the only way to know Him. We read in John's gospel, *"In him was life; and the life was the light of men"* (John 1:4). Knowing Jesus Christ is the ultimate experience of life.

Pastor Ingraham: Yes, we each need to know Him in a personal way--He is the Creator of the universe, but He is also the Savior of all who call upon His name by faith. It takes faith to believe in Jesus; it takes faith to believe in evolution; it takes faith to believe in Creation, but all those who do not believe in Jesus Christ miss the entire point of this present life—and of eternity.

Dr. Wilson: You are absolutely right. Jesus Christ says, "I am the Life"—He certainly gives real meaning to my life.

Chapter Two

Footprints In the Snows of Time

Pastor Ingraham: Dr. Baugh, I have in my hand something I am fascinated with: it is a piece of wood you have just brought into the studio. It has some very strange laminations, and it seems to be a compressed kind of wood. It is very beautiful, and I am sure it would be extremely durable. What do you call this?

An Explanation About the Ark's "Gopher Wood"

Dr. Baugh: In modern technology this is called "paralam." This particular technique was designed in Canada, and it is now produced in the United States. This is "gopher wood," and Bible students would know that gopher wood is associated with Noah's Ark.

What is gopher wood? We have for decades been trying to find out what it is. Some scholars have suggested it is white oak, some have suggested it is cypress, some have suggested it is acacia wood. That was the wood of which the Ark of the Covenant was made, and acacia wood has some lamination lines and variations in color. There are lamination lines in this piece of wood. The Hebrew word for "gopher" means "to house in," so that the structure becomes one integrated unit.

Dr. Wilson: I'm going to ask Dr. Baugh to take this further because he has just been up on Mount Ararat. That obviously is tied into the structure of Noah's Ark. I understand that observations have been made from a helicopter, suggesting that there is a wooden structure there?

Dr. Baugh: That is correct. I cannot yet divulge everything we know, and I do not want to leave a false impression that we have a piece of Noah's Ark in our hands--we do not, but we do have here a piece of gopherized wood.

Dr. Wilson: The point I want to make is: If that sort of wood came from the time of the flood, over four thousand years old, would it be fossilized? What has the concept of gopher wood got to do with it?

Dr. Baugh: In the normal processes almost any wood would have been replaced, or crystallized, and would be petrified to some degree. However, when used with seasoned wood, the process of gopherizing has already taken place: it is already compressed and crystallized. It is not petrified--it is already crystallized. That is part of the genius of gopher wood.

Whoever gave the instructions for Noah to make that ark and to use the gopherizing process must have had advance knowledge. Of course, we know who did--it was the Creator of the universe and the Savior of the world who wanted mankind to be preserved from the judgment of the flood.

Dr. Wilson: Tell us about your search for Noah's Ark.

Dr. Baugh: Dr. Don Shockey is the leader of the expedition (of which I am co-director) to Mount Ararat--we returned just a few months ago from Ararat, and we were the only research group permitted on the mountain this year.

The astronaut Jim Irwin said to an international television audience by satellite that only one expeditionary research group was permitted on the mountain this year--it was our group. We do have information that leads us to a particular spot, and hopefully in a few months, after we have been on Ararat, I will be able to give specific information relative to access to the site that has been pinpointed.

Dr. Wilson: Some time ago--perhaps three years ago--I had the great privilege of being on a threefold hook-up with Professor David Noel Freedman, one of the world's leading archaeologists, and James Irwin, the astronaut who had been up on Mount Ararat. James Irwin had some sort of experience where he actually fell off the mountain and rolled down some hundreds of feet. There were people of another nation on the mountain, and they did not want his team to rescue him...they were jamming their walkie-talkies and making life very difficult. Did you have that sort of experience?

Dr. Baugh: I did not fall, but I lost eleven pounds in three days in climbing that mountain! Ararat is the world's most treacherous mountain: it has greater electromagnetic and electrostatic energy than any other mountain on record. Dr. John Morris relates how he and his colleagues were pinned to a huge boulder by the electrostatic energy, with their arms and legs extended out into thin air. Then, too, the mountain trembles every day, and giant rocks just roll past you--hopefully they do not roll over you!

Dr. Wilson: I know from personal talks with you that some aspects of your work cannot yet be revealed. What is the nature of your research?

Dr. Baugh: Dr. Don Shockey is the repository of the information made available to us, and he was the leader of the group which we called ''Ararat Eight.'' There were eight of us in the research group, plus ground support. Eight came off Noah's Ark.

I want to make it clear that perhaps another group will find the ark before we do, and that's fine. As long as it is not an ego trip, we would be pleased for anyone to find the ark. We are not for glory, or for honor, but for our Lord's glory. Dr. Shockey designed the group specifically with that in mind: that no one would receive personal glory. Because of one aspect of the information he had, he spoke recently with a Jewish rabbi from Israel, and he said, ''Do you have any gopher wood?'' The rabbi surprised him by his answer, ''Certainly, we have lots of gopher wood.''

Don Shockey immediately asked, ''What kind of wood do you use?'' He said, ''All sorts of wood.'' Don Shockey said, ''Explain, please!'' ''Well,'' said the rabbi, ''the Hebrew word for gopher means 'to house in,' and we use living wood--you call it grafting. You have a root stock and the basic stock which is more hardy, and of course you have the particular variation you want--you pull it together and as it grafts it all becomes one unit. The cellular structure becomes integrated and there is the flow of life's systems.'' He also said, ''With seasoned wood we use various kinds of wood: we use a resin to glue it together, because resin is compatible with the grain and with the life system of the wood.'' We know that resin came from wood originally, or from plant material, and it is not exactly the same as plywood--plywood, in fact, is rather crude. ''Gopher wood is really a structural lamination process,'' the rabbi said.

That shed a great deal of light on gopher wood. This piece of paralam happens to be very superior--this particular system of laminating wood produces an extremely strong structure--much stronger than steel, yet it is resilient. A process is utilized whereby the resin penetrates the pores of the cells, and it is already unified—it is already crystallized, yet it is wood.

Pastor Ingraham: Dr. Baugh, this is very light--here we have a substantial block of wood, yet it is as light as normal wood would be--slivers almost.

Giants Not Needed!

Dr. Baugh: That says so much, because it means we do not need men eight feet tall, Herculean in their physical prowess, to carry huge timbers up to the ark. Some time ago I did a documentary with Ed Davis, an engineer who claimed to have seen two components of Noah's Ark in 1943. I believe Ed did see those components of Noah's Ark: he was taken up on Mount Ararat by Abas, with seven of his colleagues. (Abas is the name of an individual who is responsible to protect the ark--it is a very sacred structure to them.) The ark is not sacred to us: we respect it, but it is only a type of the One who is sacred to us--the real Ark who carries us across the deserved judgment upon us and our sins.

I told Ed on the telephone that our researchers at the Creation Evidences Museum had leaned toward interpreting gopher wood as being structural interlamination, so that the big beams would actually be infrastructured and laminated together.

Ed stopped me right in the middle of the sentence and said, "Sir, you are the first man who has ever said that to me, and that is exactly what I saw." He referred to the two components he had seen. They were separated by some distance, and he was over both of them with binoculars from an aerial vantage point. Ed saw jutting out from one component the members of huge beams--but those members had smaller sub-members, and the members of the others were joined. He said, "I could actually count the places where they joined--they were really small pieces of wood that were laminated together into a huge infrastructured material."

The subtitle on the sticker for this particular piece of gopher wood says, "Parallel Stranded Lumber." That is a very good description of this.

Dr. Wilson: I have been to the Creation Evidences Museum at Glen Rose in Texas many times. You are in the process of building a model of Noah's Ark there. Are you using gopher wood?

Dr. Baugh: Yes, we are building at the Creation Evidences Museum the world's largest replica of Noah's Ark--a twenty-five foot replica. You can imagine not only the parallel members around the hull and various beams, but infrastructured within that we will have the cross-members and the rooms and the compartments. The biblical Hebrew quite often begins with an abstract of what is to follow. Sometimes it is like a legal document: it covers all the bases, all the words are interrelated, such as is the case with the paralam, this gopherized product--it is interrelated. If you get a structure where even the cross-members are then infrastructured into this material, you have one of the very finest engineering techniques known.

That is really what the Creator was saying to Noah. He emphasized that the rooms and the compartments would be a part of the whole structure. So you laminate those together, and you have an idea of how Noah's Ark was constructed.

What Did Hardwick Knight See?

Dr. Wilson: When you were climbing Mount Ararat, you were, of course, making some real footprints. I think you were doing something that will be very relevant in the whole history of the ark research. The finding of the ark by others has been documented a number of times.

Over twenty years ago, when I was director of the Australian Institute of Archaeology, I was giving a series of lectures in New Zealand and I searched out Hardwick Knight, who was one of New Zealand's most respected archaeologists. He told me the story of his finding of what appeared to be part of the ark. He told me he was literally going for his life--he was very secretive about it, as a matter of fact. I think he was on some sort of secret mission.

Anyway, he told me that he could not stop, but as he moved over the snow he came across something that he described as being like an upturned gun carriage--they are the actual words he used. He had found a huge wooden structure. He kept on moving across the mountain, and it was only when he had gone a little distance further that he suddenly said to himself, ''Hey, we are thirteen thousand feet up; what on earth is that wooden structure doing there?'' He could not get back-- he would not tell me why--as I say, he seemed very secretive about it. But he had actually found up there, at a level of thirteen thousand feet, this structure that was like an upturned gun carriage. In a symbolic sense, he added to our knowledge of these ''footprints in the snow'' by telling us of his own experience as he left his own footprints there. By the way, there have been other reputable sightings. One good list has been put out by Dr. John Morris in his book, *The Search for Noah's Ark*. I want to make the point very strongly that the matter of Noah's Ark is not just a fable or legend. Those who know the facts recognize that there is something up there, probably broken into two or more parts, and it has been found a number of times during the centuries.

Dr. Baugh: That matter of what Mr. McKnight found is very logical, because apparently the ark was intact until 1840. At that time the Ahora Gorge on Mount Ararat ruptured, and one-sixth of the mountain was blown out. You can imagine the ark rumbling down the side, and it apparently broke into at least two major components. One of those later subdivided, and compartments in the foresection dismantled, and fell down the side of the mountain.

It is relevant to notice that our team, the "Ararat Eight," had some unusual credentials, and one of our purposes, if we got aboard the ark, was to examine the infrastructure and see--not only on the major scale with the large beams, but also on the minor scale--smaller pieces of wood infrastructured and laminated. We believe they were glued with the resin. Notice that natural resin is hydrocarbon-based, so it is pitch. If we are able to verify the structure is interlaminated, that will dispel all doubts as to whether or not it is the ark--this being so even if we find a minor portion of the structure.

Dr. Wilson: It is interesting that you say it will dispel all doubts. I remember that twenty years ago I was excavating in Israel; I was an area supervisor at the excavation of Gezer with the American Schools of Oriental Research, and I was talking to a leading archaeologist about the ark. He made an interesting observation, and it follows on from something you have just said: "The search for the ark is no longer in the 'funny' file." (In other words, archaeologists who have studied the facts no longer just write off the so-called legend as a lot of rubbish.) The ark has been found a number of times over the centuries.

Dr. Baugh: The evidence is there. Dr. John Morris did a good job summarizing that material and makes it clear that the ark has been found several times through the centuries.

Monastery Destroyed by an Avalanche

Dr. Wilson: Yes, it has been found over the centuries. It is important to know also that a great catastrophe took place about 1840, when one-sixth of the mountain exploded volcanically. Down at the foot of the mountain there was a monastery dedicated to the artifacts of the ark, and drawings of those are on record. This is not just something that people talk about as being "in the funny file"--it is part of history. It was there and it was known to be there. It seems that every now and then there is a whole series of hot summers and the ice line goes higher up the mountain. One result is that over the centuries the ark has been uncovered from time to time.

Pastor Ingraham: What does this mean in geological terms? This great vessel is thousands of feet up a mountain.... What does that do to the geology books?

Dr. Baugh: Possibly the mountain is rising, and we believe it is. Many mountains around the world are rising because of internal pressures and the volcanism, plus tectonic action--that involves action whereby the points of granite of the earth grate against each other, and it forces release. Tectonic plates are what the earth is sitting on--the crust of the earth, if you like.

Additionally, we can calculate back in time. We know the mountain has been at least ten thousand feet high at the time of Noah. You can imagine ten thousand feet of water covering the surface: water seeks its own level and that means we do have a global flood that actually is evidenced in geology. In fact, the implications for geology are immense. You cannot have a flood of that magnitude without it leaving traces of sedimentary deposits. That means we have to reinterpret the sedimentary deposits, not as thousands of local floods, but essentially as one major global flood. This means we must reinterpret anthropology, because every family now living around the globe would be descended from that one family that came out of that one vessel.

In addition, we should examine the facts in relation to

religion. I speak at a lot of schools where they are not too literal in their interpretation. All this evidence will affect our theology and our religious outlook, because just as we have a literal ark and there was a literal flood, so too there was a literal judgment. It follows that we have a literal accountability to a Creator, a God who not only brought judgment, but in His mercy preserved life. Theology must be restructured and returned to the biblical record itself.

If you have a vessel that is infrastructured so that things were intact, you could not get an army of men amassed around the world that could have carted it up to those heights on Ararat. It could only have been carted there by water--it could only have floated there. So we get back to the biblical account of an ark and a flood. It is important therefore to understand the facts about this type of wood--we have examined a plausible, feasible mechanism for designing such a thing, with superior wood--and it works.

Dr. Wilson: We have been talking about Noah's Ark and the flood as it is recorded in Genesis. For most of my adult life (and I am no longer a young man) I have been talking on the first eleven chapters of Genesis. In fact, if I give a lecture on the archaeological background to Solomon, the first question is likely to be, "Where did Cain get his wife?" and the next one, "How old is the earth?" So obviously I have had to study all sorts of things tied in to the early chapters of Genesis.

The longer I have gone, the more I have become convinced that that model in the Scriptures (Genesis 1-11--the so-called seedplot of the Bible) is the most fantastic, accurate presentation that the world has seen. It is a model that can be accepted if you talk about creation, if you talk even about the Garden of Eden, if you talk about long-living men, if you talk about the ark. If you come to the records from archaeology and you find that they impinge on Genesis, over and over again the archaeologists who are not "Bible believers" have been surprised how they have had to revise their thinking, and have come to realize, ''That statement in Genesis must be taken seriously after all.''

Chapter Three
Is Early Genesis Factual?

Pastor Ingraham: I am delighted to talk to both of you about this exciting subject. I would also like you to address a couple of heavy words that I am sure you can explain. I refer to "catastrophism" versus "uniformitarianism." In our schools we are usually given only one particular side--it is an incredible thing that we have only been taught one side, yet the overwhelming evidence is on the other side. I would like you to develop some other aspects of the first eleven chapters of Genesis.

Dr. Baugh: Many major scholars are rethinking and approaching the concept of catastrophism from a positive veiw.

Pastor Ingraham: Even though I was a believer in earlier years, there was a school of thought that I once engaged in that argued that the early chapters of Genesis were largely myths that had been pieced together and interwoven...that they were symbolic rather than literal. When I became more committed to my Christianity, I began to realize that these chapters are not mythology at all. They give an outline of basic fact, and if we look beyond the biblical record we find that all the archaeological evidence and anthropology dovetail into this.

Dr. Baugh: There is a tremendous body of truth and evidence supporting these early chapters. Not only that, their records are endorsed throughout Scripture. The New Testament authors, the rest of the Old Testament authors--and especially the Son of God Himself--all considered these to be literal reports of truth, and that is the highest credibility you can get. I think we are going to especially enjoy what Dr. Wilson has to say in relation to these chapters.

Archaeology Touches Genesis

Dr. Wilson: First of all, I should like to mention just a few of the ways in which archaeology touches these early chapters of Genesis. Genesis 1 starts with creation, and Genesis 2 introduces us to the Garden of Eden. There is a tablet that actually talks about the "land of Dilmun," and in the land of Dilmun the animals lay down together, the wolf with the lamb, etc. There was no problem, no sickness, no death, until a man ate a forbidden plant. It was a plant there rather than a fruit as in Eden. We obviously have something that leads back to the story of Genesis, and that ties in to the fall of man. There is the same basic concept right there.

Many critical scholars used to say, "That is all folklore." Then in the 1970s archaeologists found literally thousands of tablets at Tell Mardikh--ancient Ebla in north Syria-- and Dilmun is referred to as an actual place. I am not saying that scholars have decided it was the Garden of Eden, but it is a fact that the tablets refer to the land of Dilmun.

Actually, the story of creation is known on a whole series of different tablets--the *Enuma Elish* is a Babylonian creation series, but it is grotesque and mythological. You have the god Marduk who cuts the goddess Tiamut in half, making the heavens from one half and the earth from the other: the River Euphrates is made to flow through one eye and the River Tigris through the other. Nonsense! Grotesque! Absurd! You cannot possibly believe it!

You come back to the Genesis account and it is totally acceptable, provided you accept the concept of God.

A New Creation Tablet

We have mentioned Ebla and a creation tablet that was found there. It talks about one great being, *Lugal*, which came to mean "king," but in the early days it meant "the great one."

I was there at Ann Arbor, Michigan when Professor Pettinato from Rome told of a new creation tablet. He was what is called the epigrapher--which means the translator of the tablets. Actually I helped him to declare the fact of its existence to a group of scholars at Ann Arbor, together with details of this new tablet. I had the privilege of being there with about a dozen scholars--I was not a world leader as these other scholars were. I had been an excavator in Israel, and as I was passing I was invited to the private meeting with the excavator, Professor Paulo Matthiae, and the translator, Professor Giovani Pettinato.

We had a very nice dinner, and then a whole series of technical questions were asked. I am not really a technical person, and some of these questions were touching areas that did not especially interest me. So I thought to myself, "I am going to ask my fool question." I asked the chairman, Professor David Noel Freedman, literally a world-leading archaeologist and writer, "It has been rumored that a new creation tablet has been found. Is that so?"

It was Professor Freedman who made the news of the new tablets known to the English-speaking world, with an announcement in *Time* magazine--his picture was on the front cover. Now he simply shrugged his shoulders, smiled, and suggested that I ask ''him''--nodding toward Professor Pettinato, who was sitting next to me, with one blank chair in between. I asked Professor Pettinato if it was a fact that there was a new creation tablet, and at first he did not want to talk about it. However, with a little pressure on my part he decided to let us know what the tablet said.

Later he translated it somewhat differently, but this is the concept as he put it at that meeting in Ann Arbor: ''There was no heaven, Lugal formed it out of nothing; there was no earth, Lugal formed it out of nothing.''

At first that was all he would tell the dozen or so scholars at dinner with him there at the University at Ann Arbor, and after a little pause, I said to him, ''Sir, is there any more?'' And he said, ''Yes, there is a little more.'' Then he said, ''There was no sun, Lugal formed it; there was no moon, Lugal formed it.'' I asked him what else, and he told us that they had not yet translated the rest.

After that dinner we all went to a public lecture, and when that in turn was over, questions were asked. After that again, quite a number of people talked to the two professors in groups. At that time Professor Pettinato was again asked about the creation tablet and he put on tape the same information I have just given--he made clear what he had already told us at the dinner.

But let us go back to that dinner. When this statement about a new creation tablet was announced by Professor Pettinato, there was a pause, and obviously the scholars were stunned. Then one of them said, ''You are saying that there is a first millennium oral tradition in a third millennium written record?'' What he was saying was, ''We have always believed that the story of creation only came into the Old Testament at the time of Ezra, about 500 B.C., and you are saying it was in written form even before the time of Abraham?'' Professor Pettinato nodded his head and said, ''That is what I am saying.''

The fact is, the records of Genesis were compiled on clay tablets long before Moses' time and they were ultimately brought together by Moses. That is to say, they were compiled ultimately by Moses. There is a connecting line between the clay tablets.

There is the recurring statement, ''These are the generations of.'' That is what is called a colophon. So there is a whole series of these clay tablets, and the colophon gives the clue where one tablet ends and the next one commences.

That is not all. When we trace out those early chapters of Genesis it seems that every time it says, ''These are the generations of,'' that is the time when a particular leader dies. It is almost as though there is a funeral service, and the family clay tablets are handed over to the next in line, and he then carries on the record which eventually will again be handed over to the next in line.

Here is another interesting point. Some years ago there was found at Megiddo in Israel a clay tablet that was part of the Epic of Gilgamesh, which includes a flood tablet. It had been carried across the Fertile Crescent which goes up between the Rivers Euphrates and Tigris from Ur where Abraham used to live, and up into Israel--across to Megiddo. If that could happen about 1400 B.C. with the flood story, it could also happen with the stories of Genesis. Probably it was Abraham who carried them across the Fertile Crescent and eventually they came--many years later--into the hands of Moses.

I could go on and on--the records of early Genesis, creation, the flood, long-living men, the table of nations, and all the rest--they make beautiful sense. Even the Tower of Babel is referred to archaeologically, and scholars who know their facts today recognize that these things were written as history, as literal accounts.

Could a Man Live for 969 Years?

Pastor Ingraham: But how can we believe for even a moment that a man could live nine hundred and sixty-nine years, as the Bible says Methuselah did--how can that possibly be?

Dr. Wilson: If that was not stated in Genesis, and if it was not stated that there were giants in the earth, scholars would probably now be criticizing the Genesis record for *not* including them, saying, "The Bible did not even know that back in those times men lived for much longer periods."

There are reasons why they did live longer: the canopy surrounding the earth was apparently ruptured, and atmospheric and climatic conditions were dramatically different before the flood than they were after it. Creatures grew much bigger, and especially the reptiles which do not stop at puberty--or whatever you call it for animals--and they grew to a huge size. Humans also grew to a great size, and as we read in Genesis 2, "There were giants in the earth"; and going along with "great size" is longevity (great age) because of atmospheric and other conditions that were different before the flood.

There are also other traditions which speak of great age: the Sumerian King List, found at Kish, talks of people living for ten thousand to sixty-four thousand years--obviously grossly exaggerated, or more probably, mistranslated. It is now believed they used a system based on sixties rather than hundreds. With that correction, the total figure is remarkably close to what the Bible says. The Bible record is totally acceptable, provided we accept the concept of God. But I know Dr. Baugh can add to what I have said.

Pastor Ingraham: Yes, Dr. Baugh--what about this longevity and this huge size? How do we explain this? Some people would say this sounds very mythological?

Dr. Baugh: At the Creation Evidences Museum in Glen Rose, Texas, we are preparing to put this to the test before very long. We have over fifty consultants, each a specialist in one field or another, and they have integrated their research over a period-- for some of them now spanning in excess of thirty years. Research indicates that if you simulate the context described in the biblical record before the flood, you would have very large creatures who could live for great ages. At that time there was a canopy, a firmament shielding out the ultraviolet and short-wave radiation, and greater oxygen pressure. The fossil record also indicates that the partial oxygen pressure was greater in pre-Flood times. Men and animals were much larger, and they lived for vast periods of time. In the rocks--in the fossil record-- at least sixty percent of the life forms are larger than they are today.

Dr. Wilson: They have found a lot of new fossils over in Australia, and a leading paleontologist (he is not a Christian, nor is he a creationist) has written that, "Many of these fossils we are finding are several times larger than the species that exist today."

Dr. Baugh: That is current knowledge. Dr. Wilson has just come from Australia, and I am learning as he speaks. Let me take it further, with life forms such as the modern dragonflies with a four-inch wing span; that same life form is found in the fossil record as *meganeuropsis* with a forty-inch wing span-- they were that much larger. The rhinoceros today grows to maybe five and a half feet tall, but some years ago they found one in Germany in a fossilized form, seventeen feet tall.

The little lycopsis gets to sixteen inches tall--it is a nice little plant, and that is the best we can do today. In the fossil record it approached one hundred twenty feet in stature. Most of the life forms revealed by the fossil record were much larger. Thus there is verification in scientifically extant provable data in the fossil record to show that in the past most things were larger, and along with that would have been longevity. So we are verifying the biblical record.

The Importance of Partial Oxygen Pressure

Dr. Wilson: You just referred to partial oxygen pressure. What do you mean by this, and how relevant is it to this whole concept?

Dr. Baugh: It is extremely relevant when we consider those ancient times--by ancient we mean a few thousand years ago, in round figures five thousand years ago, before the flood. The surface of our lungs is designed so that the atmospheric pressure actually presses against very delicate membranes, and oxygen is absorbed. At the Agricultural and Mechanical University in College Station, Texas, they have a special chamber where they put medical patients with extreme problems.

I have been in that chamber twenty-two times and my wife has been there twenty-four times. They give you one hundred percent oxygen for about an hour under two or three atmospheres of pressure. What happens is this: you go in for a "quick fix"--you cannot live under one hundred percent oxygen permanently, but optimally the ratio is that you can live under twenty-five percent oxygen with two atmospheres permanently. In a short range, with one hundred percent oxygen coming into the body (but not to the level of poisoning or toxicity) the blood plasma becomes saturated with oxygen.

What that does is to cause an open wound to heal overnight. Toxins are literally removed from the deep cell tissue of the body. When you put that into living conditions, it is no wonder man had such vitality. Some researchers state that under those circumstances, with man's large lung capacity, and two atmospheres of pressure and slightly enriched oxygen, man could run up to two hundred miles without fatigue.

About Jessie McClure ...

My favorite illustration of this is the world's most famous little girl...little Jessica McClure. When she fell in the well in Midland, Texas, Jessica was there for almost fifty-nine hours. Her right foot was behind her back (because her body was so angled under those contorted circumstances) and her foot became black because of the lack of oxygen supply.

When they got her out they were not sure they could even preserve her life, and they were sure they were going to lose her foot because it had been without oxygen for so long. They rushed her to the hospital in Midland, Texas and put her in a hyperbaric medical chamber--that is a chamber with added pressure. They gave her one hundred percent oxygen because they had to have a very quick fix--you cannot live for long periods of time with that much oxygen.

They put her in a context approximating what the human body was designed to be under. They would put her in for two hours, take her out for a while, and put her back in for an hour or two. Not only did they save her life, but within a day her right foot turned pink, and then her great toe, and her second, third, and fourth toes. They lost only her little toe, and the simple reason is, her body was designed to be under two atmospheres of pressure, because under those circumstances the whole blood plasma is saturated with oxygen.

You get amazing returns in the botanical world that imbibes carbon dioxide, not oxygen. One scientist, Dr. Kei Mori of Keo University in Tokyo, Japan, experimented by adding pressure to the trunk of a normal tomato plant and he filtered the ultraviolet light.

Ultraviolet is a major problem for humans; we need it filtered. It charges the atmosphere, and we get chemical free radicals so that we are breathing and generating chemistry that is foreign to us because of that ultraviolet radiation charge.

How did the plant respond? After two years under those circumstances, with added pressure to the trunk and with filtration of the ultraviolet in the light, the tomato plant was sixteen feet tall and had nine hundred and three tomatoes on it. Our tomato plants do not live that long, or grow that big! That tomato plant does not want to die. It is now over six years old, over thirty feet tall, and it has over six thousand tomatoes on it. The tomatoes do not ripen and fall off; they do not ripen until you pull them off, so you have a Garden of Eden in a package.

In actual scientific investigation this parallels what the biblical record said all along. In other words, if you reproduce the context described in the Bible, with a canopy or firmament over the earth pressing in on the atmosphere, and if you reproduce that in scientific investigation (because water or ice, H_2O, will filter out the shortwave radiation and especially ultraviolet), you get the results that are stated in the Bible-- long-living men.

Dr. Wilson: And as the Bible also says, you would get giants! Does the Bible talk about this? And would it have any effect so far as the flood was concerned?

Polystrate Fossils

Dr. Baugh: It certainly would! The Bible uses a special word which is *raqia.* What has puzzled us for a long time is, we knew there had to be some sort of canopy over the earth because of the dinosaurs--regarded by many as the symbol of evolution, but they are really the symbol of creation.

Let me refer briefly to two different approaches to geology--they are catastrophism and uniformitarianism.

As for catastrophism: Did the flood really happen? Yes, it did! The fossil evidence points to the fact of catastrophism as a necessary conclusion. Many geologists will accept catastrophism so long as we talk about many catastrophes, not just one (Noah's flood). However, the interrelationship shown by polystrate fossils demands that we accept only *one* catastrophe. An example of a polystrate fossil is where a tree (sometimes upside down!) extends through many geological strata, even including coal.

Uniformitarianism argues that things have always continued the same way with only small changes taking place over long periods in the "geological column." Such an argument cannot be sustained--it is overturned by the factual evidence.

But let's go back to dinosaurs. They have a small lung capacity and they could not exist under one atmosphere of pressure because their lungs are so small. They could not proliferate, could not reach their full maximum potential, or even the ongoing potential for them to procreate. When those giant beasts would reach post-adolescence, they would not get enough oxygen under one atmosphere of pressure to satisfy the deep cell tissue of their bodies.

So the fact of dinosaurs demands that there had to be a greater atmosphere of pressure. The Pterosaurs, the flying dinosaurs, could not fly under one atmosphere of pressure. (That is demanded by a formula, a known ratio in aerodynamics.) Some of the flying dinosaurs had wing spans exceeding thirty-five feet.

What Is One Atmosphere of Pressure?

Dr. Wilson: Not everyone understands these terms, "one atmosphere of pressure" and "two atmospheres of pressure." You have used these terms a number of times--please explain them.

Dr. Baugh: One atmosphere is the atmosphere we have today at sea level--actually 14.7 pounds per square inch. It is the pressure in the atmosphere from the molecules and the atoms, the gases in the atmosphere. If we doubled that pressure, the oxygen would saturate the blood plasma and we would also double the capacity of aviation flight. There is a formula that has to do with density, and under those circumstances we would have life as it is described in the Bible, and the life forms found embedded in the fossil record.

The question is, "What does the Bible say about it? What does the word mean?" We have said that the word there is *raqia*, and literally that word in the Hebrew means to "compress," to "pound together," and to "stretch out" this arch or firmament, with one of its compositions being thin metal sheets.

When that interpretation was made known to us, it really threw us until further research made certain aspects much clearer. If the elements of water are put under very strong electromagnetic force, a canopy actually is held in suspension. There is what we call the Meisner Effect (levitation). Hydrogen atoms will do the same with extreme pressure, but you have to get it to two or three megabars. We are talking about extreme pressure, when it becomes super-conductive--as I say, due to what is called the Meisner Effect.

What is more, we can keep it in suspension, because tests have been run in modules showing that if you have just a vapor canopy, or a water canopy, it collapses. In order to have the context that is described in the Bible, and as well as the ancient world (especially the fossil record), it has to be a literal stretched-out canopy with metal-like components. The first place it is mentioned in the Bible is right here in Genesis 1.

Pastor Ingraham: Then the Bible and true science correspond exactly at this point?

Dr. Baugh: Yes. The Bible has anticipated modern science in a remarkable way.

Chapter Four
Did Man and Dinosaurs Walk Together?

Pastor Ingraham: I want to talk about something that boggles my mind, and that is the concept that man and dinosaurs once walked the earth together. Did they leave their footprints in the stones of time at the same time? Dr. Wilson, let's start with you. What about this idea of men and dinosaurs walking the earth together--do you believe they did?

A Surprising Phone Call

Dr. Wilson: It blows your mind, doesn't it? I was founding president of a college in Australia, Pacific College of Graduate Studies--and our degrees are available in America. I have been coming to the United States regularly for many years now.

Years ago I got a telephone call from Dr. Baugh, ''Will you come over to help us dig up some dinosaur and human footprints?'' I just said, ''What are you talking about?'' and he replied, "We have found dinosaur and human footprints together!" I said, "I am not convinced about that!" He simply said, "Will you come over?"

I have been an excavator--I was an area supervisor at the excavation of Gezer in Israel with the American Schools of Oriental Research--which is possibly the world's most prestigious body in archaeology, and I have excavated elsewhere. So he pressed me: Would I come? I said, "Look, it's a long way from Melbourne in Australia over there to Dallas in Texas." He said, "I'm paying the fares." And so we talked some more--this phone call from America to Australia was at his expense!

When the bank check arrived to pay for my airfare I knew that he was serious--so I came over, and eventually I arrived at Dallas-Fort Worth Airport. I was met at the airport by a good friend of all of us, Pastor Ronald Jenkins. I was taken to his home at Duncanville for a little while, and then we drove to the "dig." There were two areas being excavated: Dr. Baugh was in charge of what we called Locus A, and I was in charge of Locus B, *locus* meaning "a place."

We got organized and then he said in passing, "We have the press coming next Wednesday." I asked, "What are you going to tell them?" He responded, "We have written to them all over America and told them to come and see what we are doing--they will see human and dinosaur footprints together." I was astounded--"You have put that out in writing?" and he smiled, and nodded his head, "Yes!" I thought to myself, "This is the world's Number One optimist!"

I have been a university professor in both Christian and secular institutions, and I was a director of archaeology for quite a number of years. So I said to him, "Carl, I am an academic! I am not going to blindly identify with you on this--here we are on Friday saying that by Wednesday you are going to say that here are dinosaur and human footprints together…Carl, what are you doing? That is terribly risky, and I have to tell you that I cannot identify with it unless I am personally convinced.'' But let Dr. Baugh go on with the story.

Dr. Baugh: By Wednesday Dr. Wilson himself had truly participated in the procedure--hard physical work, by the way. This was on the Paluxy River, near Glen Rose, Texas, and that is where the Creation Evidences Museum is located (I am its director).

As Dr. Wilson has indicated, he was not satisfied even when I first called him. He told me so on the telephone as I spoke with him, he in Australia and I in the United States; and he said it again when he arrived--"Carl, if I am not personally convinced, and if I do not see first-hand evidence, in no way can I identify with any statement to the press that the evidence is here." I said, ''Fair enough!'' and I told him details of how we had already excavated four human footprints and twenty-three dinosaur prints on the same layer we were now excavating.

So by the next Wednesday Dr. Wilson had actively participated in helping to remove the twelve-inch overlay of stone. We do not just go in there, find an exposed area, and see what trenches may have been cut, or what intruders may have carved. We actually remove the twelve-inch layer of limestone and then delicately excavate through the four to seven inches of clay marl, and then the depressions are very clear.

Wilson Becomes Convinced!

By that next Wednesday, before the day was out, there were eight separate press agencies looking over our shoulders, some of them simultaneously. A number of scholars had arrived from across the country. As we excavated we continued to find a trail of prints, and the beautiful thing is that at Locus B, Dr. Wilson--assisted by a fine gentleman, Joel Nickmeir, from St. Louis, Missouri and his son Cliff and others--had removed the stone, and had delicately excavated a beautiful dinosaur footprint, seven and a half inches from a very clear human footprint.

It had the great toe, the four other toes, the ball, the arch, the heel calcaneous section. The human footprint has three arches, and all of these arches were there: the medial arch, which is the standard arch, the metatarsal arch, which runs under the foot, and the longitudinal arch along the outside. There was a curvature, and when we look back over the photographs, all three of those arches were there. So Dr. Wilson had done what we had already been doing, with findings that had convinced us.

So the press arrived, and I will let Dr. Wilson say what he then said to the reporters after he had excavated firsthand not only a dinosaur print but a human print, seven and a half inches apart.

Pastor Ingraham: May I just ask this: The significance of them being side by side is that they had to be made at the same time?

Dr. Baugh: That is correct! Limestone is actually concrete calcium carbonate. We have eight different geologists who are part of our consultant base, and they all verify that limestone is of the same elemental constituency as concrete. Concrete does not harden due to pressure in time, but cures or lithifies, and limestone cures or lithifies by a chemical reaction which causes a heating, and then a diminishing--and it is cured. You can cure it in a matter of hours! You can go as far as thirty-six hours in the process, but it has to be very rapid, and additionally we have found with what are called polystrate fossils (these are fossils that extend down into one layer and up into the next layer) that there was a cycle to the whole thing.

Dr. Wilson: If you have a stratum of limestone and then mud and clay and more limestone strata--and find that you have one of these fossils that extends up through the lot, clearly it could not possibly just grow there. It has to be encased in the various strata, and therefore the catastrophe must be a sudden, simultaneous thing.

Out Goes the Geological Column

Dr. Baugh: That is so--it must be while the fossil is still intact. For instance, it might find a branch while it is still intact, while it is not decayed. We found very tender plants like lepidodendron, extending from one limestone stratum through marl into the next limestone level.

Dr. Wilson related to the press that at one time he had held to the concept of the geological column but this sort of evidence rules it out as a valid index of time.

One lady, the head of her department from the *Fort Worth Star-Telegram*, interviewed Dr. Wilson at length. He told her, "There was a time when I held to the concept of the geological column, but no longer." Then she said, "What are these prints?" and he said, "These are human footprints!"

Dr. Wilson: I remember the incident very well. She also said, "How do we know you aren't faking all this?" I said, "Come on down in the clay, in the mud, and see for yourself!" There is an awful lot of mud around when you have a river that has been flowing and you remove this clay and marl. So she took me at my word and got down into the clay and said, "What is your technique?"

If you know what you are doing, the technique at such an excavation is really fairly straightforward. You simply remove the clay and you come through to the white of the limestone. Then you go across the limestone--you just simply get rid of what's on top of the uncovered limestone--and suddenly the color changes.

As a matter of fact, this is the same principle in all sorts of different areas of archaeology. The color changes and you say, "What's this?" I let that lady see what I was doing, not with the particular prints we have just referred to, but with another dinosaur print. She was actually able to see with me that if you went in with your trowel you could fairly easily remove the clay and you could not remove the limestone--that is like solid concrete--it is absolutely set. So she was able to see that we were not faking it. All we were doing was removing the clay carefully, and then when the clay was removed the outline of the footprint was there--whether it was human or dinosaur. We uncovered both on this ledge--they were there. She had to be convinced by the evidence firsthand--and she was. And she wrote us up very favorably indeed.

Pastor Ingraham: Is it safe to say that you gentlemen brought creationism out of the abstract and back into the concrete?

The Concept of Evolution Destroyed

Dr. Baugh: Well put! That is very true. But let me take you back to another point.

You asked a moment ago the significance of finding human and dinosaur footprints together. In another book that Dr. Wilson and I co-authored called *Dinosaur*, we give statements by leading evolutionary scholars. They admit in print that if we can verify academically, with good background proof, that man and dinosaur lived together, it totally destroys the concept of evolution. The point is, here man appears with what is interpreted to be a primitive form in geological strata that are said to be a sign and age of about one hundred and eight million years ago. Now if man existed here, without precursors leading up to man's appearance, then he had to be created. Whether the time is as the evolutionists claim, or it be recent, he had to be created--either way that is the position.

Precursors are previous forms leading up to the present. However, there are no forms leading up to man: he simply and suddenly appeared on the scene. There are no transitional forms, no missing links. Man appears suddenly in superior form--and superior is correct. We have excavated many tracks that demonstrate all this. In the last eight and a half years we have found fifty-seven human footprints, one hundred and ninety-seven dinosaur footprints, a major dinosaur, and we have a fossilized human finger that was brought to us from these limestone ledges.

Dr. Wilson: I have seen and handled that finger, and believe me, I accept it as being human. You have already heard that I am somewhat of a skeptic until I have the evidence right in front of me, but in this case I did not need any convincing. Dr. Baugh set out to convince me it was a human finger--I mean, there it is! I am not an expert on human fingers, but it was clear--it was about the second finger and it has turned out to be the ring finger of the left hand. What is more, I'm told it was a lady's finger. By the way, in the main you can even decide with feet whether they are male or female. Dr. Baugh, you know more about that than I do--would you comment?

Dr. Baugh: The gender can be identified in the main, taking averages. For instance, the proportionate measurements of the heel to the front of the foot vary between males and females. The human finger I've referred to has the fingernail intact. We sectioned it: I had nineteen different medical experts observe it, and all of them said it is specifically a human finger, and some of them were even able to identify its gender from various factors.

So we have men and dinosaurs living contemporaneously. Some of these human footprints are so clear that we are able to identify not only the great toe and the second toe, but the fact that the second toe was depressed and the other toes curled slightly.

If you know anything about the forward locomotion of man, you know that with a normal forward movement you spring forward, your great toe remains extended for dexterity and balance, and the other four toes actually curl to add some spring. We are finding that, and due to the pace and stride between the tracks we are able to determine the agility of the individual. Now that we have the human finger, we are able to determine certain aspects of the health of the individual. We are able to determine the lady's general health because in this "specimen" even the epidermis (the outer skin) is preserved.

Now someone will raise a red flag and say, "How do you get soft skin texture preserved?" Under the right circumstances it can be preserved, and in our museum we have a fossilized earthworm that was originally a lot softer than a lady's finger. It was preserved perfectly, properly tapered, and the various segments can be seen. All this is no problem under the right circumstances.

How Is Something Fossilized?

Dr. Wilson: What circumstances? How do things fossilize?

Dr. Baugh: It must be fossilized rapidly. Fossils are not being formed today. In our atmospheric context living organisms die or are killed, and bacteria begin to attack them immediately, and they deteriorate--and, of course, scavengers get them. They are designed to float upward, and unless they are buried immediately you will not get fossilization. They must be encased very rapidly and essentially buried as they are dying in material (not sand) that will encase them, as in a vault.

Dr. Wilson: Can I tell you a story…at the end of that particular excavation in 1982 at Glen Rose we came to the very last day. It is a strange thing known among archaeologists that often something important is found on the last day. It is almost uncanny, the way that has happened.

This particular day, Dr. Baugh and I happened to have stopped excavating--that is, I had, and I walked around from Locus B to Locus A where he was working. I still had my trowel in my hand and Charles Hiltibidal, our field supervisor who was in charge of the machinery, came on down and said, ''I think there is a scratching up on the top level there. Would you mind if I took the backhoe and dug out some of the overburden?'' Between us we said something like, ''There's no point in doing that Charles. That's the top stone stratum of the earth's surface; you will never find anything there--forget it!'' And he said, ''Well, I have this feeling that there is something there, but it is buried under all this overburden. In any case, we've paid a lot of money for this backhoe and it's just sitting there. Let me go up and try!'' So Dr. Baugh said, ''All right, Charles, you go on and do it if you want to.''

Dr. Baugh: Let me add something before Dr. Wilson gets to the climax. We do not normally excavate with a back-hoe. We just use the backhoe to get close to the spot we are interested in, and then we hand-remove the material. But I had such little faith in finding anything on that top layer that I said to myself, ''It won't hurt; the tires of the backhoe are rubber, and you can remove that silt and the pleistocene soil (as it is called in paleontology).'' So I said, ''Yes, go ahead!'' We would not have been able to use the backhoe at Locus A. So Dr. Wilson and I simply said, ''Sure, take the backhoe!'' We had very little confidence that Charles would find anything on that top level of the earth's surface!

Dr. Wilson: So Charles Hiltibidal got on the backhoe and started to remove that overburden. It was irregular in height and we estimated it was about six to eleven feet stretching over the limestone. Charles moved about forty feet up, across and back from the edge of the Paluxy River.

Soon we had forgotten about Charles as Carl Baugh and I worked away on a particular problem at his Locus--I was temporarily away from my own area a little further upstream. Then Charles Hiltibidal came back to us and he said, ''I think I've got a dinosaur footprint.''

Six "Impossible" Dinosaur Footprints!

I happened to be the one with the trowel in my hand at that time, and so we went back up there to this top stone stratum of the earth's surface. I had the privilege of removing the marl from the limestone to which Charles had now got down through the overburden. Then I had the real privilege of excavating six dinosaur footprints--left, right; left, right; left right! They were approximately three and a half feet from each other--even though you know the approximate distance, it varies slightly, of course. You have a fairly good idea where to go after you've found the first footprint, for you simply stride it out and remove the mud and marl until you come to the clean limestone. You get rid of the clay from the limestone that surrounds it, and it is a nice sensation to find the clay removing and the outline of footprints coming to light beneath your feet-- footprints that have not been seen in thousands of years until you uncover them.

So I found these tracks--and I am stressing "I" for a particular reason. There was no doubt that they were normal dinosaur prints, such as those that have been commonly found along the ledges of the Paluxy River. There have been many of them found in the area of Dinosaur State Park, not very far downstream from the McFall site where we were digging. The recovery procedure was photographed. There was just no way this excavation could be other than genuine.

The point of telling that is that some time later, in one of my further visits to help out at the excavation, a leading Christian who is a very fine scientist met up with me--we had known each other previously. He has written a highly acclaimed scientific textbook and he told me, "Your finding of those dinosaur footprints on that top stone stratum has been written up, and they said it was one of two things: Either the Indians carved them into the limestone, or you faked them."

So those were the two possibilities! Let me just make

this point: Dr. Baugh and I went together to a particular university lecturer in Indian art and we asked for all sorts of details about what the Indians did--how they understood their artwork. We were told quite clearly that they do not carve into stone; they will go to the side of a cave or just inside the cave, and there they do their paintings. They do not carve across stone like this!

Another point is: how could they manage to carve all these things underneath all that overburden, that topsoil? The fact is, these critics say that the footprints were fakes. Did the Indians crawl underneath? Or did they excavate all the overburden and then put it back over their carvings? Fakes? The idea is preposterous and ludicrous. Talk about an ostrich burying its head in the sand--these are modern scientists, so-called, who apparently are unwilling to face facts that oppose ''sacred cows'' of uniformitarian geology.

We have even been told that the human footprints down there are actually those of visitors from outer space--that they were made by astronauts from another planet!

The point of insisting that these were fakes is clear. The dinosaurs supposedly died out seventy to one hundred million years ago--in a stratum lower than this top stratum. This top stratum, according to uniformitarian geologists, was thirteen million years old. (We do not accept that of course; we accept a date that is much more recent.) Therefore, they argued, the dinosaur just could not have been there ''only'' thirteen million years ago--so they had to be fakes!

I want to make this point very clearly: If they were fakes, I am the person who faked them--and I did not fake them! God is my Witness, and others were present also. I went down there and I used my trowel, with people watching and photo-graphing, and I actually have a cast of one of the prints. I personally uncovered six dinosaur footprints on that top stone stratum--and they were not fakes. It showed that the dinosaurs were there, ever so much more recently than most uniformitarian geologists would allow. These dinosaur footprints were on a higher level than human footprints we had found, and therefore the dinosaurs had to be there after those particular humans whose footprints we had uncovered.

Pastor Ingraham: Is it not then a question of the will? Isn't this a case of seeing the truth in that old expression, "Man convinced against his will, is of the same opinion still," which is the blindness that we constantly deal with in terms of the Gospel.

Dr. Baugh: There is hope for individuals who will turn to God. It requires repentance. We have witnessed a world-class scholar, Dr. Clifford Wilson, who because of his academic background had a mind set against recency. His mind was set against humans and dinosaurs living contemporaneously. We have heard his own testimony--how he was convinced by the evidence. I am sure that there are many who would receive full assurance from God Himself if they would honestly address these convincing evidences.

Pastor Ingraham: Is it not incredible, how time keeps running out...time is one of those elements that we have been getting close to in these talks in this series, *Footprints and the Stones of Time.* We have talked about the footprints, we have talked about the stones, and next let's talk about this matter of a time frame.

Chapter Five
All About Time

Pastor Ingraham: I am sure that you two scholars will help many people come to a more definite commitment to the credibility of Scripture. You show that Scripture is far more accurate than most people have ever realized.

We have talked about footprints--both dinosaur footprints and human footprints, especially in limestone formations. These stones were not something that existed and then just eroded--you believe they formed as a result of a cataclysm that is identified with the flood of Noah's time.

We have also said that the element of time is very important. Dr. Wilson, how does the time element fit into all this? And how do we account for the fossil records so far as time is concerned?

Dr. Wilson: Let me give a personal explanation: I was in the United States some twenty years ago, working for my Ph.D. I got it a little bit late in life--I am no longer a young man! At the same time I was providing for myself and my family by lecturing in one of the very well-known Bible colleges, one of the best in the United States. I went there with a very real sense of call, but it was also possible to work towards a hard-earned secular Ph.D. I was lecturing in archaeology and Old Testament studies, and I had about ninety students in this particular class. I was explaining that it did not matter how old you thought the earth was--that the Bible allowed for that, and so on; I was confident that you did not need to worry about this ''young earth'' business.

A student came to me afterwards and asked, ''Sir, have you ever read any of the writings of Professor Thomas Barnes?'' In honesty I had to say, ''I've never heard of him.'' ''Well sir, if I brought you some of his material, would you read it?'' Out of courtesy, I said, ''Yes, I'll glance through it.'' He brought to me an article dealing with the depletion of the earth's magnetic field. This started me on a journey. I found that there were really serious arguments for an earth that was only a few thousand years old.

According to Professor Barnes, the depletion of the earth's magnetic field involves a half-life of about fourteen hundred years, in round figures. Then I was introduced to a man who had done some investigations of Dr. Barnes' work for one of the leading scientific investigative institutions in the United States. I asked him, ''Did you investigate this material of Professor Barnes?''

''Yes.''

''What conclusions did you come to?''

He responded, ''Well, it's interesting material.''

I asked him, ''Did you prove him to be wrong?''

''No, we could not prove him to be wrong.''

''Well, did you therefore accept what he had to say?''

He looked at me and then commented, ''Well, you are not talking about me; you are talking about the organization I represent.''

I said, ''Yes,'' and he then told me, ''No, it was not accepted.''

I asked, "Why not?" and he answered, "Because the attitude was, we know that the earth is four billion years old and therefore this material cannot be right."

Dr. Barnes was tackling an evolutionary concept dear to the heart of leading members of the scientific establishment. "He could not be right," was the attitude. Satellites have since shown that the half-life to which Professor Barnes refers (he was at that time professor of physics at the University of Texas at El Paso--he has since retired) was even less than fourteen hundred years, making his case even stronger.

Eventually I tracked down Professor Barnes; he has become my friend--I have stayed in his home. One night we were walking there at El Paso, and his wife was walking with my wife. I said to Professor Barnes, "Tom, I am not a physicist, and I do not understand some of what you've told me. I don't understand all your equations. Will you tell me, how old is the earth? Maybe fifty thousand years?"

And I can hear him right now! He said, "Fifty thousand years? Ho, ho, ho! By that time the earth has long since blown up!"

The fact is, certain heat effects double every fourteen hundred years (or less). If you go back from where we are now, back by that figure of fourteen hundred years, we would double that heat effect. In another fourteen hundred years beyond that, we would double it again. It doesn't take much imagination to see that before very long the earth would indeed blow up! It would only take a few thousand years.

A Journey Of Discovery

The point is, that led me personally into a journey into a whole lot of other fields, such as in the field of astronomy. Again, I am not an astronomer, but Dr. Baugh and I could talk at length with some of the quotes we have about astronomy from scientists. For instance, we now know the rate at which clusters of galaxies are moving away from each other. Gravitational pull is involved, and because the rate at which they move away from each other can be measured, we can therefore extrapolate and say, "When did they start to move away?" We find it is only a few thousand years--not the millions of years so many scholars have talked about.

There are many other arguments like this that lead to the conclusion that the earth and even the universe can be measured in terms of thousands of years, and not millions or billions of years. Even the light traveling from the nearest star no longer needs to be talked of in terms of vast periods of time. Another way of measurement is possible--using what is known as the Rymanian Effect--giving only a very short period of time. At the very least, people should take seriously the possibility that the earth is young. I personally have come to the total conviction that the earth is only a few thousand years old.

I also believe that one of the most interesting arguments for recency comes from the Paluxy River in Texas. I personally have been there with Dr. Baugh many times and he should tell us about that, because he is the leader of that team. A trilobite, supposedly dated to five hundred million years ago, was found in the same ledge system where he has been excavating--not exactly the same spot, but in the same ledge system where he and his team have been working. The curator of the Sumervell County Museum at Glen Rose who found it with her mother insists that she also found dinosaur footprints right there. So you have the trilobite that supposedly died out five hundred million years ago and the dinosaur that supposedly died out one hundred million years ago. I have personally found (with Dr. Baugh) dinosaur and human footprints together. Just immediately before that we had removed the limestone ledge of twelve inches, with cameras clicking--there was no possibility of fake.

Then, of course, there was the finding of the dinosaur bones, upstream from the McFall site but in the same ledge system at the Paluxy River. Evidence shows us that these various creatures were around at the same time, and that they are recent.

Pastor Ingraham: Dr. Wilson, what intrigues me about all this is that scientists for a century or more have been able to date the layers of the geological strata by the types of fossils that were found in them. How do we explain that?

Circular Reasoning!

Dr. Wilson: We have already referred to this briefly. We explain it by two simple words: circular reasoning! In investigations such as those about evolution, nobody can be an expert in all fields. Thus geologists depend on biologists for expertise in a particular area--and so the geologists accept the dating that the biologists give for their fossils. The biologists likewise then accept the dating that the geologists give to the rocks in which the fossils are found--so we have circular reasoning.

Pastor Ingraham: They date the fossils by the rocks and the rocks by the fossils?

Dr. Wilson: Yes, but let me say straight away that it is not a matter of non-integrity. It is the fact that each is not an expert in that other field--some scientists are not necessarily men of integrity, but in the main it is simply that they are trusting the conclusions of scholars in the other science. Nevertheless it is certainly circular reasoning, because these creatures from supposedly different time periods are there in the rocks together. Genesis 1 talks about the land creatures being created on the sixth day of creation and man was made on that same day--they were all there together. The geological column is *not* a reliable index for dating.

Pastor Ingraham: How do we account for the fact that there are complex organisms on one layer and not so complex organisms on another layer?

The Order of Fossils--Including Humans--In Rocks

Dr. Baugh: That is a very good question! First, all life is complicated. The trilobite is supposedly near the very bottom in the layering--given five hundred million years of assigned age by a standard geologic interpretation. However, it has both a compound and a simple eye. In many respects its eye system is more complicated than the cameras that were used when men walked on the moon. In some respects it is more complicated than man's eye. A complex, compound system and a simple eye system are combined in what is supposed to be the very earliest life forms. Life itself is very complex, and this humble trilobite is another reminder of that.

There is a plausible explanation as to the general tendency for simpler life forms to appear early in the so-called geological column. There is a general tendency to find the sea-dwelling creatures lower, to find reptiles next, and then to find creatures that would be mammalian. They would be rather sluggish, and then come the more agile mammals, and finally we have man. In fact, with his intelligence, man would escape the first aspects of the catastrophe more easily than lesser creatures would.

Under flood conditions in the days of Noah you would have this same general scenario. Creatures that were in the water already, living there, would be covered first as the tremendous silt and cataclysmic tidal impact brought up the new material expunged from the earth as the fountains of the great deep were broken up. It would cover some of the great sharks, and would also cover some of the sea-dwelling life that did not want to move at all--they would just get caught. Then reptiles, which were not afraid of water (amphibians particularly--creatures that could live both in or out of water), would very quickly be engulfed. Then the larger, more sluggish of the mammalian creatures would get caught, and then the more agile creatures that could run better and escape a little longer under more general circumstances. Finally man would be engulfed, despite his reflexes and his ingenuity and ability to work out how to escape. The Bible makes it clear that the mountains were covered. There was no place to hide.

Another reason why there aren't as many humans as lesser creatures found in the fossil record should be pointed out. If a deer or a man (or some mammal) got caught early in the flood, unless silt and deposit covered him completely, there would be a tendency for his body to reach a higher level. We need to remember that the metabolism, the gaseous chemistry of a mammal, causes its body to bloat and then to float. So it is that even if he got caught along with the ''lesser'' mammals, the amphibians, the reptiles, the sharks and everything else, he would probably not be encased in mud as they might be.

In addition, you have what is called geographic zonation. Some creatures prefer an area just by reflex--that is, away from the water; they are mountain or hill creatures.

Then you have specific density. Some of the fossils have been measured as to specific density: some drop to the bottom, but some float and have a measure of buoyancy in water. So there would be a general tendency for certain levels to be appropriate for some creatures and less so for others. That explains part of what we see in the geological column, yet it is also true that those cataclysmic activities would have occurred in one series of events of less than one year.

Here is the bottom line: According to evolutionary theory trilobites were supposedly in the very early stages of development and then died out a few tens or hundreds of millions of years later. However, they are found along with the intermediate layers, that is, the intermediate life forms by evolutionary interpretation (such as the dinosaurs), and in that same layer. Thus you find the ultimate life form, man, together with what is supposedly the earliest forms, and this removes all time from the calculations associated with the geological column. This means that those hundreds of millions of years mean absolutely nothing...all these life forms existed at the same time!

Millions Of Years?

Dr. Wilson: I think we should comment further, too, about carbon dating; lots of people say, "We read about millions of years"--and so on. Dr. Baugh has talked about the canopy being ruptured, and the partial oxygen pressure being dramatically changed. One result, among other things, is that you simply cannot presume that you have what we call "constants" back to the time of the flood, and that these constants continue. It is not possible to say with certainty, "We recognize that this is how long ago things lived, because we are able to measure it by this system involving the half-life associated with carbon dating. Even if carbon dating is accurate for five thousand years, as is often the case, that does not mean we can assume that our investigation will be accurate beyond that point. The dramatic changes that took place, with different atmospheric conditions at the time of the flood, mean that the measurements earlier than the flood of Noah's time are irrelevant--they simply do not count.

In any case, carbon dating can be used only for a matter of thousands of years; after one half-life (about five thousand, seven hundred and thirty years) the dates go all over the place. Yet carbon dates have been given to coal! When I was a boy at school they used to tell us that every layer, every stratum of coal, took about two million years to form. Now carbon dates of about five thousand years have been given to coal, and the vast majority of things for which carbon dates have been given show recency--much against the expectations of scientists who expected that radiometric dating of various types would point to much longer periods of time.

Pastor Ingraham: It is said that it takes millions of years to form stalactites and stalagmites...how do you answer that if the earth is only a few thousand years old?

Dr. Wilson: Let me first tell you an experience, and then let Dr. Baugh add to what I say. I was in New York in the subway, and we stopped at one of the train stations there and I simply reached up and pulled down this stalactite, some inches of it. According to the argument you have just put forward about millions of years, that stalactite had to take a vast period of time to grow, yet at the time I pulled it down, the railway subway had been there for only forty years! This is a very good illustration of the fact that we do not have vast periods of time at all. It was a stalactite, but it was there in the subway, it had grown in the subway in only forty years.

Pastor Ingraham: So these stones of time that we have been talking about don't point to long ages and yet they are the supposed scientifically established basis of the scientific establishment. Apparently we have been led down a path that is totally fallacious?

Dr. Wilson: The Scriptures say: *"Having eyes, they see not; having ears, they hear not."* That still applies today. The evidence for creation that is recent is overwhelming. I am embarrassed almost to say this, because I used to teach in many parts of the world that you could forget the need to think of a recent creation, that it did not matter how many millions of years were involved. I was a Christian, but I believed in this concept, close to theistic evolutionary approach. I didn't call it that--I called it "progressive creation." I was wrong, and the evidence is very strong that the earth--and the universe--is only a few thousand years old. The evidence comes from many areas of knowledge.

Do You Teach Creationism?

Pastor Ingraham: Dr. Clifford Wilson is the founding president of a Christian college in Australia.

Dr. Baugh: Yes, Dr. Wilson is the founding president of Pacific College of Graduate Studies. It has been established for eleven years and scholars of international reputation have lent their names to it.

Pastor Ingraham: Dr. Wilson, what do you teach? Do you teach creationism?

Dr. Wilson: Yes, we teach creationism. Pacific College of Graduate Studies has been active in Australia for eleven years, and we have become a body that is taken very seriously. We have had, and we still have, hundreds of students, and we recently have been able to register in the United States, in the state of Missouri. Most of our work is external, with correspondence courses. However, believe me, we are not a ''degree mill.'' The leading scholars who identify with us make that clear. One of the states of Australia has approved our courses for students coming to study in Australia. Our courses are in good shape. And, yes, when it comes to these areas of Genesis, we simply teach creation. When it comes to the inerrancy of Scripture, we teach the inerrancy of Scripture, because that is what we believe.

Pastor Ingraham: Let me ask you one other question about the time period that we have been talking about. I heard you make a remark some time ago, Dr. Wilson, that President Carter asked for a report that touched on the date of creation. Would you tell us a little bit about that?

Dr. Wilson: It is simply this, and I think Dr. Baugh might give you more details: President Carter asked for a report which was basically, "How old is the earth, and how old is the universe?" Eventually the report came back, and included in it (among many technical aspects) was a statement something like this: "If we wanted to, we could fit the whole of the dating into the time period demanded by the dating system of Bishop Ussher." (Bishop Ussher was the man who said the world was created in 4,004 B.C.) I am not saying I accept that--I am simply relating what Bishop Ussher said, and I do not necessarily say "I accept that." The scientist was saying, "If we wanted to, we could fit it all into the framework of about six thousand years."

Dr. Baugh: We have a statement about this on the wall of the Creation Evidences Museum in Glen Rose, Texas. The director of the High Altitude Observatory in Boulder, Colorado, is a man with impeccable degrees in standard academia, and he directed the program. He had a colleague in England, and together over a period of years they measured astrophysically the demise of the sun, and they found that the sun was shrinking. They worked with the recognized parameters and the evidence available and they found they could not deny that the sun was shrinking. Their calculations at that time showed that it was shrinking at five feet per hour--and that is amazing! Since then they have tried to adjust that figure. They assumed that there were bursts and recessions on the size, but that simply is an assumption. Even if the rate of shrinking is only a percentage of that figure of five feet per hour you would still come to a startling conclusion of recency.

For the sake of the exercise, let us take that rate of five feet an hour. That would mean that if you extrapolate back six thousand years ago, which roughly is the time of creation according to Ussher's calculation, the sun would have been very large. If you go back much further than that, you get into real trouble. For instance, if you go back one hundred thousand years at that rate of demise, the sun would have been so large that it would have pulled the earth on to its surface because of its gravitational attraction. In going back you add the energy of the sun, and the mass of the sun, and the electromagnetic field as well--the sun has an electromagnetic field. Of course, one hundred thousand years is only a drop in the bucket in evolutionary time.

Let us take it even further than that. The standard evolutionary interpretation is that eleven million years ago Ramipithecus was spawning forms that later developed into man--that is a standard anthropological evolutionary teaching. If you have the sun shrinking at the rate of five feet an hour, eleven million years ago when Ramipithecus supposedly was around on earth as a lower primate, the actual circumference (that is, the actual outside dimension of the sun) would have come all the way out to the orbit of the earth. That, of course, is absolutely impossible! The earth would have been obliterated long since.

The Bible Shows Dinosaurs And Man Were Contemporary

So when we look at the facts it becomes clear that those elements of time that are speculated by evolutionary theory are really introduced because of a pre-conceived notion, a humanistic evolutionary interpretation. The fact is, those elements of time are not there when we examine them.

Let me give one final statement. What we have talked about--and particularly about human and dinosaur cohabitation--is not new. It is found in the biblical record. In Genesis 1 we learn that on the fifth day of creation great whales were created, great sea creatures and some of the water dinosaurs, and marine creatures. On day number six, God created the rest of the physical creation, such as the mammals and the dinosaurs. Man was also created and then, before the day was out, God created a mate for him. And God always does it right.

So the introductory chapter of the book of Genesis shows man and dinosaur living contemporaneously. In Job 40:15 the statement is made, *"Behold now behemoth [the dinosaur], which I made with thee; he eateth grass as an ox."* Man and dinosaur did live contemporaneously--the Bible tells us so.

Part II

Footprints In Stone

Convincing Pictorial Evidence

brought together by
Dr. Clifford Wilson

Dr. Carl Baugh Uncovers a Dinosaur

As Dr. Carl Baugh carefully brushes some of the evidence, we notice that this particular dinosaur actually formed part of the earth's stratum at that point. The dinosaur was overwhelmed and compressed down into just a few inches. This was not a slow process over a long period of time, but something that happened catastrophically. There seems to be no model to explain this and other phenomena other than the massive destruction brought about by the flood of Noah's time.

"Footprints and the Stones of Time"—according to the reproductions at Dinosaur State Park—bring us back over millions of years. We shall present another point of view.

We visit Dinosaur Valley State Park on the Paluxy River at Glen Rose, Texas. We shall examine some of the paintings and diagrams at various sites around the park.

There are various types of dinosaurs, usually classified by their hip structure. Naturally they leave different types of footprints in stone.

The two main orders according to the hip structure are Ornithischian, which is regarded as the bird hip dinosaur, while the Saurischians are supposed to be the lizard hip dinosaurs. However, no forms in between reptile and bird have ever been found.

Wall murals at the Dinosaur State Park Museum depict dinosaurs in their habitat of long ago—dramatically different as to food supply from what would be found in Texas today.

They did not only eat at the same place, but they fought together as well. Here n Acrocanthosaurus with its small arms is supposedly attacking a Brontosaurus.

The Stegosaurus was well plated—they did not have "rocks in the head," but it does seem they had rock-like structures just about everywhere else.

Then there were the Ankylosaurs, and these were thoroughly protected along the lines of armored war vehicles today. The varieties are amazing!

Then there were the Ceratopsians, the horned dinosaurs. You would certainly need to swing into a high tree if one of these charged you!

The Theropods were meat eaters, and quite a number of their tracks have been found in the Dinosaur Park area.

The Sauropods were among the largest of the dinosaurs, and again many of their tracks have been found in Dinosaur Park.

The Ornithopods were a duck-billed variety, and they too have left their visiting cards in the forms of tracks in the limestone.

Interesting attractions in the park are the fiberglass copies of Brontosaurus and Tyrannosaurus Rex. The long neck traditionally associated with this Brontosaurus has now been shown to belong to another dinosaur.

Tyrannosaurus Rex has a massive display of teeth. His little front limbs are in dramatic contrast to his huge rear legs. Probably he used those little limbs to tear up dead animals—it is possible that Tyrannosaurus Rex was a major scavenger in the dinosaur family.

Here Dr. Clifford Wilson is crossing from the far side of the Paluxy River to the museum side of the Dinosaur Park.

A sign nearby tells us that these three toes are impressions left long ago by one of the many dinosaurs whose "visiting cards" have been left in this state park.

Famous naturalist Roland Bird found many dinosaur footprints in the state park area—before it was declared a state park. Some of those footprints have been transported to this place just outside the museum.

Dr. Wilson points to a footprint found by Roland Bird. Dr. Bird also referred to casts of human footprints he handled. He rejected the evidence of his own eyes—the "Establishment" view was that dinosaurs died out 70 million years ago and man has been around for only 2 million years.

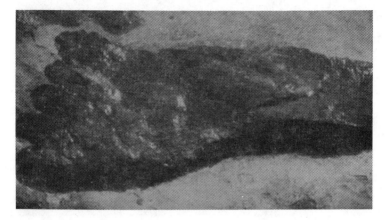

Other footprints besides those of dinosaurs have been left in the state park. This one is so plain that the unbiased observer has to acknowledge that it was indeed human.

This print is not very much bigger than the foot of the 20th century man whose foot is suspended over the impression in stone.

Now we find dinosaur footprints, and a human footprint at the bottom right. The only reason for rejecting it as a human print is the "Establishment" argument that dinosaurs had died out long before man was around.

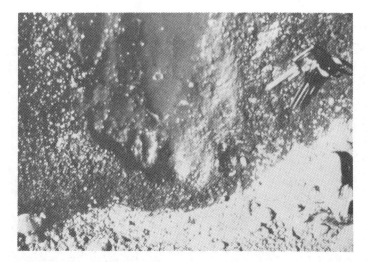

This time it is a left foot we are looking at, and the keys on the right side of the picture will give you an idea of the size of the footprint. The evidence has become so compelling that the whole idea of dinosaurs and man walking together must be taken seriously.

Again we see the impression of a human foot in Dinosaur Park. Such footprints become weathered; this is natural once the limestone is removed by flash floods or by humans. After exposure, changed atmospheric conditions soon cause deterioration.

Here a modern foot is placed into that impression in stone—this time with the water scooped out. The visitor from long ago was a larger person, but the feeling was that the basic pattern was the same.

We have come away from Dinosaur State Park, not very far upstream to the McFall site. It is a beautiful area, especially when the river is gently flowing as in this scene with Dr. Clifford Wilson in the foreground.

The limestone strata are typical of supposed levels forming part of what is known as the geological column. However, the evidence is that these are sudden deposits, not set down over vast periods of time, but laid down catastrophically at one particular time.

This is the evidence of a flash flood which actually took place while an excavation was proceeding further upstream. The Baugh team literally had to get out quickly. Local people know that a flash flood sweeps all before it.

Even a few days after the flash flood had subsided, the devastation is still horrendous. It is common to see limestone ledges that have been shattered by "natural" happenings.

Flash floods are a major reason why the limestone has been smashed up and down the banks of the Paluxy River.

After such flash floods, evidence has been forthcoming for the last generation, with both dinosaur and human footprints uncovered at times.

Here we have outlined the shape of a dinosaur footprint with water for photographic purposes. This dinosaur was moving toward the ledge at the very top left of this picture (before the ledge itself was laid down).

In the left center we see dinosaur prints leading up to where Clifford Wilson is pointing. This is one such footprint just before it would have gone underneath the ledge at his back. Dinosaur footprints are found at a whole series of these ledges, on top of each other.

One method of the Baugh team was to remove limestone ledges, with the permission of the ranch owner (the late Emmett McFall). He is seen at the right back of this picture.

Here a ledge that is 12 inches deep is being manhandled off to the side of the Paluxy River. It was known that there would be dinosaur footprints underneath, because they led right up to the edge of the ledge.

Sure enough there was a dinosaur print there, but a few inches away was a human footprint as well. Dr. Carl Baugh is pointing to the human footprint on the left of the picture, only inches from a small dinosaur's impression.

Dr. Baugh is holding the measuring tape while Field Supervisor Charles Hiltibidal is holding the tape at the other end. A dinosaur and a human footprint are approximately 18 inches from each other.

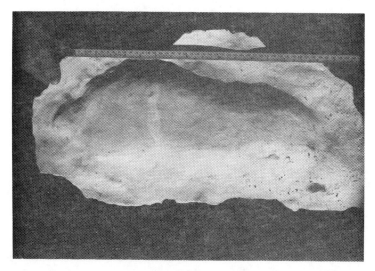

Here we have a series of pictures that have been excavated by the Baugh team. This one has only the great toe showing clearly, the others having been broken off over time. The shape of the foot can clearly be seen.

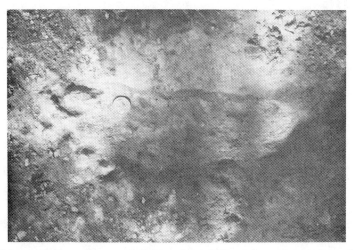

This particular picture was taken about 300 yards upstream from the McFall site, and on their own time members of the Dallas State Police took this cast. They were emphatic that it could be nothing but a human footprint.

This is a photograph of the "Miller" footprint, taken just as soon as it had been cleared. Once again the five toes can be seen clearly.

Many people across the world with a size 11 shoe have put their foot into a copy of this "Miller" cast owned by Dr. Clifford Wilson, always testifying that they felt reasonably comfortable. (There are variations of shape according to width.)

Notice where the fingers are at the top of this cast—showing where there is a piece of jutting rock, about 1/2 inch below the second toe, which can be clearly seen in the picture. The shape of the footprint is clearly seen.

Here is another cast, this time taken by Dr. Clifford Wilson.

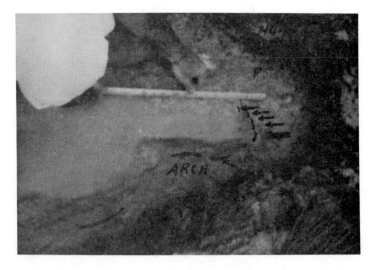

Sometimes humans actually trod into dinosaur footprints. They were racing through setting limestone, not just wet mud. There would be some coolness in the water associated with the dinosaur's imprint, and it would not take much effort for intelligent people to walk into those same tracks.

Here is another evidence that humans sometimes walked in footprints left by dinosaurs. The human footprint is at the right side of the picture, and our "model's" finger is pointing to the large toe.

This is one of a series of footprints in the Taylor Trail. It also is a footprint inside a dinosaur footprint, and indeed in some of the series there is a dinosaur footprint, an adult footprint, and a child's footprint as well.

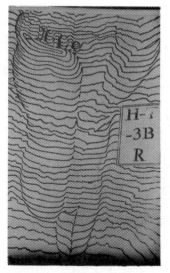

Don Patton has shown there was a human print as well as a dinosaur print in this impression. The human print can be seen on the left, and the dinosaur print extends to the bottom of the picture and over the letters H-T. The evidence has convinced several previously skeptical scientists.

This is known as the Kasatchie print, having been taken from sandstone in Louisiana in June 1989. A number of people have brought footprints and other impressions in stone to the museum.

This is the Burdick print, purchased many years ago by geologist Dr. Clifford Burdick. It has been sectioned with his permission, and the geological report is that it shows all the geological features of a genuine human footprint.

The evidence is not confined to human or dinosaur footprints, for about three miles upstream the Baugh team found the bones of at least two dinosaurs. Here Dr. Carl Baugh is examining one of the bones.

Dr. Baugh is carefully measuring two femurs. This is the first time dinosaur bones have been found in the same stratum as dinosaur footprints on the North American continent.

Here is another picture of some of those dinosaur bones when they were first excavated. Experts from various museums have come to the site and testified that they are indeed dinosaur bones.

Here is just another view of the dinosaur bones. These were compressed from probably 20 feet high to about 8 inches by the pressure that was suddenly thrust on them when they were overwhelmed.

The hand brushes in the picture give some idea of the size of these massive creatures from the past.

Dr. Baugh carefully scrapes away some of the clay that had become attached to a dinosaur bone. The bones of two dinosaurs were found, and possibly there are others still uncovered.

Local people believe that men and dinosaurs walked together some thousands of years ago. This man demonstrates the distance between the remnants of two human footprints in the Paluxy River.

Dr. Carl Baugh (on the left) talks with Mr. Grover Gibbs, recently retired postmaster at Glen Rose, pointing to one of the footprints that local people have cemented into a suitable place for exhibition near the post office.

Local resident Slim Adams is the son of George Adams. His father found many bones in Panther Cave, several miles away but still in the Paluxy River area. Slim has had them in his freezer for many years!

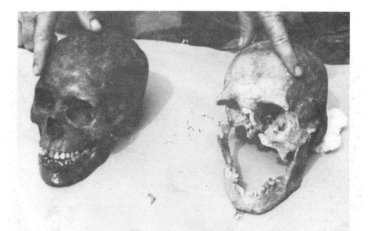

Here are two of those skulls. It is believed by the measurement of the bones that the larger of these would have belonged to a woman over 7 feet tall. Local people do not know to what period the bones should be dated, merely suggesting that they are in a "prehistoric" period.

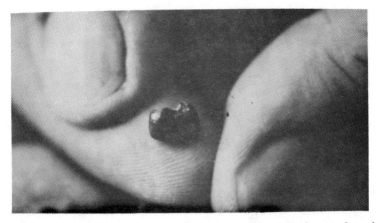

University professors compared this tooth to fish and other teeth and suggested that this tooth is one of them. A leading dental surgeon listed **10 points of sameness to show this is actually part of a human tooth.**

This fossilized finger, shown alongside a modern lady's hand, was found in the limestone at Glen Rose, though not by the Baugh team. Alongside it is a fossilized trilobite, found by local "rock hound" Beatrice Moss in the limestone ledges at a tributary of the Paluxy River.

Local people are convinced dinosaurs and humans walked together. James Backer's family is so convinced. They tell stories of various modern animals having been found at the same levels as dinosaur bones in nearby gravel pits.

The family of the late Mrs .Emmett McFall has donated this photograph showing her with a human footprint modeled to illustrate large human tracks like those excavated on their farm.

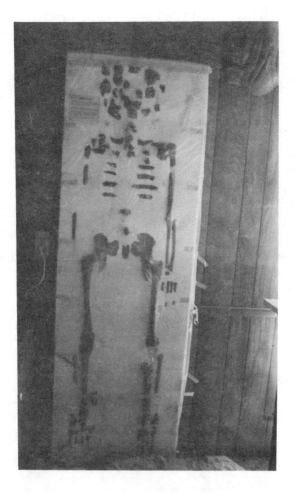

Then there is Moabite Man. Dr. Carl Baugh was told of this find in Cretaceous stone at Moab, Utah, and the bones have now been brought together and are on display at the Creation Evidences Museum at Glen Rose. Some critics have objected that the bones are not really ancient, but the evidence of their findings and the dating of the stone means that they should be accepted as authentic. If it were not for their relevance to the creationists' position, there would be no argument about their validity.

The same is true of this man-made hammer found in Cretaceous stone at London, Texas. Chemical analyis has demonstrated that the find is all that is claimed for it—a man-made object in relatively recent times, but encased by stone that is supposedly many millions of years old. Obviously the stone itself is also recent.

The hammer is man-made, and it had to be in existence before it could be encased by this Cretaceous stone. The stone is supposedly millions of years old—but clearly it cannot be, for man has been around for only a relatively short period of time.

Other objects have been found embedded in coal at other sites—including jewelry and a bronze bell.

Man-made artifacts encased in stone or coal are convincing evidences to the recency of both man and the enclosing material.

This giant ammonite has been donated to the museum. A modern ammonite is shown on the right. Dramatic climatic differences, including increased oxygen pressure, meant that man and animals would be much larger in earlier times.

This is a footprint of the late Max Palmter, a modern giant. Dr. Baugh's hand is alongside. Many fossil finds today are reported to be several times larger than their modern counterparts.

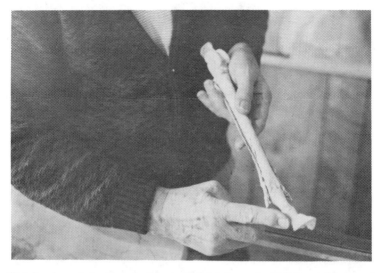

This is a horse's hoof, and even the humble horse has left its visiting card in fossilized form, demonstrating that it too lived at the same time as other creatures such as dinosaurs and—yes—humans.

This saber-toothed tiger would tell the same story if he was able—that he lived and walked with a creature called man, and with others called dinosaurs.

At the Creation Evidences Museum at Glen Rose there is a cast of one of the so-called archaeopteryx specimens. Until recently it was claimed that this was a "missing link" (or in more recent terminology, a "transitional form") between reptiles and birds. However, as a specimen of archaeopteryx has been found in the same level as fully-fledged birds, the argument has been totally discredited. (There have also been fakes associated with archaeopteryx. However even accepting this one and others as genuine, there is no evidence whatever that these are transitional forms between reptiles and birds.)

Put simply, the archaeopteryx was supposed to demonstrate the gradual evolution of reptiles into birds. It had some reptilian features but it was fully feathered. However, some of those supposed "reptilian features," such as claws on its wings, are also possessed by some modern birds such as the ostrich, and others of those features are not to be found in a number of modern reptiles. We repeat there is no fossil evidence for in-between forms. The wings of archaeopteryx were fully developed—and indeed it had several types of fully developed and functional feathers.

Dr. Gary Parker states, "Actually the final piece of the archaeopteryx puzzle (for the time being, anyway) was put into place back in 1977. That's when James 'Dinosaur Jim' Jenson (who is famous for finding the huge dinosaurs called 'Supersaurus' and 'Ultrasaurus') recovered the femur of a bird in the same rock unit in which archaeopteryx is found. What does that mean? It simply means that archaeopteryx cannot have been the ancestor of birds, because birds already existed" (*Creation: The Facts of Life*, p. 101).

This is a cast of footprints that Dr. Mary Leakey found at Tanzania, East Africa. The scientific world accepted the evidence that what she presented is indeed evidence of human footprints, but they have no problem with this because there is no argument that they were at the same time as dinosaurs or other creatures supposedly dating back many millions of years. The evidence of footprints presented in these pages is far more convincing. The evidence of human footprints at the Paluxy River should be accepted, and indeed will eventually be accepted.

Mary Leakey's son Richard is now recognized as a world-leading paleontologist. He has acknowledged that widely held views about human evolution have been disproved—and he has nothing to offer in its place (*The Battle for Creation*, Creation Life Publishers, 1976).

The September 1986 edition of *Discover* is *very* revealing. It includes an article entitled, "Baffling Limb on the Family Tree," by Pat Shipman, listed as "paleontologist at the Johns Hopkins School of Medicine."

The editorial comment at the beginning of the article tells us that "an ancient and confounding skull, with enormous teeth, massive crests, and a tiny brain, has cast the pre-human lineage into disarray." The last paragraph is indeed startling. Dr. Shipman tells us: "We need new fossils more than ever, as well as a re-examination of our old ideas. I don't think the new synthesis will come quickly, for most of these choices will make many of the primary researchers in this field uncomfortable. Changing your ideas is more painful than moving a house, but the results are also more exciting....Like an earthquake, the new skull has reduced our nicely organized constructs to a rubble of awkward, sharp-edged new hypotheses. It's a sure sign of scientific progress." It is yet another indication that the theory of evolution is in disarray.

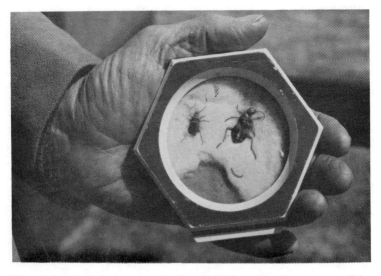

When Job talked about creatures that could throw fire, he was not talking folklore, myth, or legend. The bombadier beetle is renowned for its capacity to throw fire at the predator that sets out to devour it. Job talked about dinosaur-type creatures throwing fire (Job 41:19-21).

Tommy Bass, a lecturer at the Creation Evidences Museum, is here holding one of the dinosaur footprints that an interested friend donated to the museum. They come in many shapes and sizes.

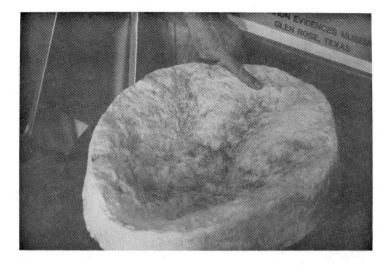

This is a larger dinosaur footprint at the Creation Evidences Museum, very similar to the many tracks to be found up and down the river, not only in the state park area, but in the banks of the Paluxy River over a considerable distance. They are usually badly weathered, unless recently uncovered.

The same sort of evidence comes from other countries. In this case, these are three dinosaur footprints literally found way overhead in the ceiling at a mine at Mount Morgan in Central Queensland, Australia.

In a previous book, *Dinosaur—Scientific Evidence That Dinosaurs and Man Walked Together*, Drs. Baugh and Wilson showed that six dinosaur footprints were uncovered on the top stone stratum of the earth's surface at Glen Rose in 1982. Here in 1984 Mrs. Avis Wilson, wife of Dr. Clifford Wilson, is showing that over two years considerable weathering has taken place. In fact, the track had to be uncovered again to show where they were under the debris.

This sort of evidence is important—easily seen, and yet not sufficiently appreciated. The uncovering of dinosaur footprints did not just commence in 1908 when modern reports highlighted such finds. The Paluxy River would have had flash floods for centuries, leaving massive destruction in earlier as well as later times.

The evidence of weathering of tracks is easy to see up and down the Paluxy. Clearly these creatures were around relatively recently—certainly not *millions* of years ago. The weathered tracks point to that. The weathering of this track—in just two years—is a clear pointer to recency. These "footprints in the stones of time" were made by creatures who were brought into being on the sixth day of creation, at the same time as man (Gen. 1:24-26).

Dr. Clifford Wilson in 1991 is again pointing to those same tracks first uncovered in 1982. They are much less clear now than previously. They have had to be uncovered and outlined with water to show where and what they are. The tracks had become almost obliterated over only nine years of weathering. It is simply wrong to suggest that these tracks would have been around for millions of years. It just does not fit the physical evidence.

Critics claimed that these could not be genuine because (by "Establishment" dating) they were on a stratum that was "only 13 million years old." Dinosaurs supposedly died out 70 to 100 million years ago—these prints "must be fakes."

Dr. Clifford Wilson personally excavated them after an overlaying cover of overburden (topsoil), between 6 to 11 feet deep, was removed.

Witnesses—with cameras—watched as the prints were uncovered.

The evidence is conclusive. These dinosaurs were around much later than the critics allowed. And as they were on a stratum ABOVE human footprints (as well as on the SAME stratum as other dinosaur and human footprints), dinosaurs and humans were indeed contemporary.

Dr. Carl Baugh is in the center of this picture and photographs are being taken of a lepidodendron at the McFall site. It is interesting to notice that this plant extended into two different strata of limestone. One often-quoted evidence of the various strata of the earth being brought together in a short space of time is the fact of polystrate fossils—fossils that run through several strata, as is true in this case for two strata. This plant could not have grown through the limestone. It had to be there first, and encased as the setting limestone swirled around it. It is very clear evidence of the fact that the strata would have been laid down suddenly, and virtually simultaneously. We have every reason to believe that the flood of Noah's time was responsible, and that the swift tides, perhaps separated by only about 12 hours each, would have caused the separate strata to be laid down.

Ultimately we are brought to the conclusion that *one* catastrophe—not many—was responsible for the sequences of polystrate fossils around the world.

The same evidence was seen with the dinosaurs recovered about three miles upstream. Here famous American artist Robert Summers is helping to excavate some of those dinosaur bones. Notice that the bones literally form the stratum at this particular point. The limestone is interrupted by the dinosaur bones, and then the limestone ledge continues. This dinosaur was forcibly overtaken, and was actually encased by the encroaching limestone with tremendous pressure, so much so that what is believed to be a 20-foot Theropod was condensed to about 8 inches. This offers evidence of a cataclysmic happening, causing the sudden death of this huge creature from the past.

This dinosaur was uncovered by the Baugh team, and its genuineness has been attested to by various university authorities.

If it were not for the implications supporting creation, it is possible that funds would have been available for a major excavation. It might well be that this area is a veritable dinosaur graveyard—with other animals also entombed by the great catastrophe associated with the flood of Noah's day.

GEOLOGIC TIME TABLE

ERAS	PERIODS	CHARACTERISTIC LIFE FORMS	
CENOZOIC	QUATERNARY: RECENT EPOCH, PLEISTOCENE EPOCH	RISE OF MODERN PLANTS ANIMALS AND MAN	25,000 1,000,000
	TERTIARY: PLIOCENE EPOCH, MIOCENE, OLIGOCENE, EOCENE, PALEOCENE	RISE OF MAMMALS AND DEVELOPMENT OF HIGHEST PLANTS	12,000,000 25,000,000 35,000,000 60,000,000 70,000,000
MESOZOIC	CRETACEOUS	ANGIOSPERMS AND INSECTS ABUNDANT, FORAMINIFERA PROFUSE, AMMONITES DINOSAURS BECOME EXTINCT	70,000,000
	JURASSIC	FIRST REPTILIAN BIRDS, LARGEST DINOSAURS, FIRST PRIMITIVE ANGIOSPERMS	
	TRIASSIC	EARLIEST DINOSAURS, FLYING REPTILES, MARINE REPTILES, AND PRIMITIVE MAMMALS, CYCADS AND CONIFERS COMMON, MODERN CORALS COMMON, EARLIEST AMMONITES	200,000,000
PALEOZOIC	PERMIAN	PRIMITIVE REPTILES, EXTINCTION OF TRILOBITES	
	PENNSYLVANIAN	EARLIEST KNOWN INSECTS, SPORE PLANTS	
	MISSISSIPPIAN	RISE OF AMPHIBIANS	200,000,000
	DEVONIAN	GREAT VARIETY OF FISHES, FIRST AMPHIBIANS	TO
	SILURIAN	EARLIEST KNOWN LAND ANIMALS, RISE OF FISHES	500,000,000
	ORDOVICIAN	EARLIEST VERTEBRATES, PRIMITIVE LAND PLANTS	
	CAMBRIAN	BRACHIOPODS TRILOBITES WORMS ALGAE AND CORALS	
PRE-CAMBRIAN		OLDEST KNOWN LIFE - MOSTLY INDIRECT EVIDENCE	500,000,000 TO 1,800,000,000

We go back to another of the charts at the Dinosaur State Park, and it tells us about the geological timetable, running through periods that supposedly go back 1.8 billion years, right down to only 25,000 years ago with the rise of modern plants, animals, and man. The evidence against this geological column has been devastating, demonstrating that the geological timetable should be thrown out. Instead, the evidence is that the various strata of the earth, from so-called pre-Cambrian to Cenozoic times, should be recognized as being laid down at the same time.

Notice that trilobites are shown in the Cambrian strata, at the lower end of the Paleozoic era—200 to 500 million years ago.

Then notice that dinosaurs supposedly became extinct at the time of the Cretaceous strata—70 to 200 million years ago.

At the top of the scale man is listed, together with modern plants and animals—only 25,000 to 1 million years ago.

Yet trilobites, dinosaurs, and man each left evidence in the Glen Rose limestone ledges of having lived together. Genesis 1 makes far better sense than the out-dated geological timetable.

A visit to such places as the Grand Canyon in Colorado shows the way the various strata are formed. It is almost as though they have been put there with a sharp knife. These various strata did not slowly merge together over vast periods of time. They were put down suddenly, resulting from one great catastrophe. We have seen that the evidence of polystrate fossils is very relevant: it shows by interrelationship that it was one great catastrophe, and not a great series of catastrophes.

The geological evidence from the Grand Canyon points to vast quantities of water—not just a gradual erosion from the relatively small Colorado River way below (as many geologists have claimed). Collapsed strata can be seen at various points, with the same strata continuing again on the other side—hardly the result of that little river meandering through the gorge!

Fossil evidence from the gorge itself—such as trilobites in the "wrong" stratum—again point to life forms co-existing rather than being separated by vast ages.

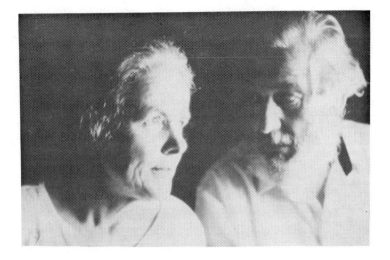

Here are Dr. and Mrs. Arthur Wilder-Smith. Dr. Wilder-Smith has three earned science doctorates, and has been widely acclaimed as an expert in a number of areas associated with creation science. In *The Origins*, one of the film series for Films for Christ in which he is featured, he points out that the geological timetable depends on the rocks to date the fossils, and the fossils to date the rocks. He makes it clear that such circular reasoning is hardly good science.

At Glen Rose he has expressed himself as satisfied with the conclusions that men and dinosaurs did indeed walk together—and that the Baugh team has found authentic human footprints.

Other scholars have acknowledged this problem of circular reasoning. Here is one relevant quote: "Contrary to what most scientists write, the fossil record does not support the Darwinian theory of evolution because it is this theory (there are several) which we use to interpret the fossil record. By doing so, we are guilty of circular reasoning if we then say the fossil record supports this theory" (*Compass*, "Paleontology and Uniformitarianism," May 1988, Vol. 45, p. 216).

Scholars have changed their mind and become convinced as to the recency of creation as they have faced the facts objectively. This is Dr. John Leslie holding part of a dinosaur's spinal column that was recovered at the Paluxy river. Dr. Leslie was on faculty at Monash University in Melbourne, Australia. He came to fellow faculty member, Dr. Clifford Wilson, asking for creation evidences because he was unsure of what to believe. He carefully studied the evidence made available, and became convinced and forthright in his commitment to the Genesis creation record. (John has since returned to the United States for further post-graduate studies.)

That experience has been multiplied as scholars have come to examine the evidence at Glen Rose for themselves. Many have come with an open mind, especially wanting to know the truth because of the vehement objections to the possibility that dinosaurs and men walked together.

Literally dozens of scientists, many with Ph.D. degrees from accredited universities, have now lent their names to the belief that dinosaurs and men were indeed contemporary. The evidence is conclusive.

At the Dinosaur State Park Museum one wall chart talks of findings dating back to 105 million years—we reject that most vigorously. The evidence is that both dinosaurs and men were on earth only a few thousand years ago. The millions of years demanded by evolutionary scientists simply do not fit the facts as they are found alongside the Paluxy River in Texas.

Dating that gives vast ages is subject to serious challenge. An example is given by Malcolm Bowden in *Ape-Men—Fact or Fallacy?* It mentions Richard Leakey's 1470 skull.

"In July 1969 Richard Leakey sent samples of volcanic tuff to London for dating the '1470' skull which he had just discovered. Using the potassium-argon method of dating, they gave a date of 220 million years, which was an impossibly high figure for the emergence of man's ancestors. On receipt of further samples of tuff, crystals which appear fresh were selected and gave an age of 2.6 million years, which is the figure now used for this fossil" (*Ape-Men—Fact or Fallacy?*, M. Bowden, Sovereign Publications, Kent, 1977, p. 66).

"All these methods however are based upon a number of presumptions, some of which cannot be verified. It is assumed that:

"(a) There were no products of decay already present when the rock was first formed. Thus, if, originally there was argon in a rock as well as potassium, it would appear very old even at the start.

"(b) None of the original radioactive material has been leached out at any period. Both uranium and potassium can be leached out of rock. Even in granite this leaching can occur in significant quantities. In one instance an iron meteorite lost 80 percent of its potassium by having distilled water run over it for 4 1/2 hours.

"(c) None of the products of decay were lost or gained during the course of time. There is evidence to show that argon will diffuse from areas of high pressure to those of lower pressure. Argon will migrate from the lower rocks to the higher ones, giving the latter an appearance of great age...."

The conclusion from all the evidence is that men and dinosaurs did live together—at the same period of time, only a few thousand years ago. When man's wickedness was overwhelming, God also was overwhelming in judgment—the judgment of Noah's flood. But those people in the ark were secure with God's protecting hand over them. "Footprints and the stones of time"? Yes, they point to another ark, another way of salvation, and sercurity in Jesus Christ. He said that if the children did not praise Him, the very stones would cry out His praise.

The stones of archaeology have cried out as the integrity of Scripture... and the limestone ledges of the Paluxy River in Texas also continue to cry out as the the integrity of that wonderful book, the Bible. Jesus said, *"Thy word is truth!"* and that truth starts at Genesis 1, continues on through Genesis, and goes on to the very last book of the Bible, Revelation. And its central theme is still Jesus Christ, the Rock of our salvation.

Part III

Time, Stones, and Early Genesis as the Seedplot of the Bible

Chapter Six
The Paluxy River Mystery Is Solved

by Dr. Carl Baugh

A great mystery has been solved! Since 1910 the Paluxy River basin in Texas has been an area of controversy. In 1908 the first dinosaur footprints in modern times were found in the bed of the river after a spring flash flood ripped up the ledges of limestone. After the waters had receded, huge prints were found, some of them in triangulation form, tridactyl form, which later were assigned to a particular dinosaur called Acrocanthosaurus. Some of the other prints found were more oval in shape, and were definitely made by a creature such as a Pleurocoelus, a great Sauropod dinosaur.

These days there is no doubt that dinosaur prints have been found in the Paluxy River basin. In fact, within a five-mile radius of Glen Rose you can find numerous dinosaur footprints if you simply look far enough on the right ledge, or dig far enough and remove enough stone.

In 1910 local resident Charlie Moss found a trail of tracks at the McFall property, in the bed of the Paluxy River. He found these after the spring floods had ripped up a layer of limestone, and after the waters had receded. These tracks had very clear definition to indicate that they were of human origin. The man whose prints were found had been walking, and then he increased his pace and stride as if he started to run: in fact, Charlie Moss verified that when he ran the tracks were just about six feet apart.

The tracks were about fourteen inches in length, indicating that the individual was of a stature in excess of seven feet. That means that even without running he could reach a six-foot pace and a twelve-foot stride with no difficulty. All this fits into the indices of the human anatomy. In addition to this, Charlie Moss verified that these tracks in the bed of the Paluxy River, which he ascribed to human origin, had the relevant human details. Some of them had all five of the toes, others had a trench and a great toe. Anthropologically this is very consistent with the human anatomy and forward locomotion. They had the ball, the flange, the medial arch and the heel: all of this was ascribed and accredited to the discovery of the late Charlie Moss of Glen Rose, Texas. Now the intrigue continues.

Human and Dinosaur Footprints Together

Emmett McFall discovered a number of these prints along with dinosaur prints on and near his property, adjacent to and in the bed of the Paluxy River. Then Jim Ryals removed from the McFall property what was claimed to be the very best human footprint ever seen in these ledges, as good as the Burdick print. The Burdick print was taken from the area somewhere in the Glen Rose district in the 1940s, and it was purchased in an Arizona rock shop by Dr. Clifford Burdick. He was assured that it, along with the dinosaur print that he purchased, came from the Paluxy River basin of the Glen Rose area.

Recently geologist Don Patton and I researched the area and we traveled up and down numerous tributaries to the Paluxy. We were working on these tributaries because the Creation Evidences Museum is in possession of the Burdick footprint. This has been termed (in print) by the opposition-- that is, the humanistic community--as being a perfect human print; in fact, it is called such by Roland T. Bird.

Four years ago *Natural History* magazine ran a special ten-page article in which they referred to the Burdick print as a perfect human print, but obviously a carving.

Don Patton and I cleared up the first mystery of the Burdick print in that, in a cross-branch tributary to the Paluxy, we found a layer of limestone which has all of the identifying marks of the matrix of the Burdick print. It has some crystalline inclusions--some little pockmarks made by a creature that was encased and later deteriorated, and this is of significance because it identifies the matrix structure and the surface structure of the Burdick print.

Additionally, we took some of the stone of this layer in the cross-branch to Cordell Van Huus, a professional apiaderist. He sectioned it, and the microstructure is identical in nature to that of the Burdick print, and the consistency of it is identical. It cuts exactly the same with the saw. Cordell Van Huus has verified that he will put his professional reputation on the line-- that it really is the very same stone.

Thus we have solved the first mystery in identifying a layer of limestone in the Glen Rose area--it is slightly different from the normal limestone in the Paluxy River itself, but we have found it in the Paluxy River basin area.

Now the second mystery has been solved. The Burdick print was a perfect print, in that it had the great toe, the second, third, fourth and the little toe. It had the ball, the flange, the medial arch, the heel, and the lateral arch, and even a slight bulge at the base of the fifth metatarsal.

It had some problems: it is slightly wider in the flange, all five of the toes are splayed forward. At Loma Linda University they sectioned across the wide flange and ball area some years ago, and they could not find lamination pressure indications underneath.

So even among creationists there was a mystery. Was it a carving? Local resident George Adams (not to be confused with his scholarly brother Ernest "Bull" Adams) had admittedly carved a few human prints, and a number of dinosaur prints--was this one of them? We certainly did not think so, for a number of reasons. On the Burdick track there is a carving line showing where the print originally started. However, they had to extend beyond that original carving to cut it out of the matrix. So they certainly did take it out of the matrix of stone, and that would mean that the print was in it originally. Also the mud between the great toe and the second toe pushed higher than any other portion of the track. It would certainly be a rare fortuitous combination of circumstances for the track to be carved in material and the mud between the great toe and the second toe to be pushed up higher than the rest of the print. On the other hand it would be consistent with normal activity in pliable mud if the print were genuine.

The width of the flange is no problem. That was indirectly illustrated by Professor Tuddle, writing in the March 1990 issue of *Natural History* magazine. He shows a photograph of his foot in comparison to a native's foot from South America. The native was accustomed to walking barefoot, and the flange of his foot was forty-six percent of the length of the foot; the Burdick print shows the flange to be forty-eight percent of the length of the foot, indicating very close agreement. So it certainly is within the range of human width compared to length.

It is relevant to add that I have undertaken detailed research from the literature, and the indices showing the width and the length ratio make it clear that the Burdick print certainly is within the range of human footprints.

Was the Burdick Footprint Genuine?

Now we went further. In our research at Glen Rose we wanted to really solve the mystery: was the Burdick print genuine? We had found a layer of stone identical to it, thus verifying that it came from the Paluxy River area. However, along the one section, across the flange and the ball of the foot, we did not find laminations.

In our research we found that when you move forward in the normal forward locomotion of the human pace and stride, you place a great amount of weight on the heel, transfer a portion of that to the outside lateral portion, transfer a major portion to the inside, to the ball and great toe, and you spring forward with the great toe extended and the four other toes curled in the spring--that's the normal forward locomotion. Yet the Burdick print did not have the curl to those other four toes--it had them splayed. Since it is a right print, this would indicate that the individual was making an adjustment in direction. In other words, he was turning left--he was angling to the left. In order for the toes to be splayed like that it would also indicate that the pace was not a normal extended pace, but a shortened pace. That would be normal if you changed direction, so that the weight was borne in the interior portion of the foot, with all four of the other toes splayed and the great toe extended as usual. This would mean that in the ball and flange area you would only get a balanced distribution: the greatest weight should be in the heel and it should be under the toes.

So we went to Cordell Van Huus again, sectioned the heel of the print, and found very definite lamination distortion pressure lines under the heel. So it was a genuine print--but we went further. Twice he sectioned the anterior portion under the great toe and through the other toes: once in the central area and once under the ball, the smaller toe and the extension of the great toe.

In each case we found that under the great toe there were very definite distortion lines of pressure in two directions: underneath it, and the turn to the left--the position to the left. We found under the other toes very definite lamination pressure lines. We also found between the fourth and fifth toes a curl in the mud between the toes, which now of course was stone. This would be consistent as the foot was adjusted and pulled slightly to the left in the forward locomotion, with an adjustment to the left. Thus there is no question that the Burdick print is genuine. That mystery was solved.

The Mystery of the Taylor Trail

However, the greatest mystery involved the Taylor Trail. The Taylor Trail is an entire trail of prints that had originally been discovered by Jacob McFall over forty years ago. Then in 1960-61, Rev. Stan Taylor came to the Paluxy and extended the Taylor Trail under the ledge of limestone, removed the limestone, and followed the trail. Nine prints were observable at that time--some of them he had found, and some of them had been discovered by Jacob McFall. He found by excavation that there were human footprints in the bed of the river where the Ryals print was, and where there were trails of dinosaur prints.

So it was that Films for Christ made the splendid *Footprints in Stone* film. It was used internationally as the greatest tool for the creation explanation. It showed very definitely that the entire geological column was fallacious, beginning with the early Cambrian, the Paleozoic, going through the Mesozoic, and the age of the dinosaurs, accentuating the Cretaceous period where one hundred and eight million years ago, according to the standard evolutionary interpretation, the dinosaurs roamed the mud flats at Glen Rose; extended up through the Cinozaic era and finally to man.

Stan Taylor showed very clearly that this entire geological column was in error, and man and dinosaur lived contemporaneously. That totally disrupted the geological column and upset the entire theory of evolution. In fact--as D.H. Milne and S. Schafersman wrote specifically in 1983, in the *Journal of Geological Education* on page 111, about the reports of finding human footprints and dinosaur prints together--such an occurrence would seriously disrupt conventional interpretations of biological and geological history, and would support the doctrines of creationism and catastrophism.

We certainly agree that such would be the case. So the question is very important: Are there human footprints among dinosaur prints?

So it was that the celebrated trail to be examined was the Taylor Trail. While *Footprints in Stone* gave data regarding other footprints, the trail for the central evidences of the film-- totally disputing the evolutionary concept--was the Taylor Trail.

Then in August 1984, Ron Hastings and Glen Kuban, two researchers, went to the bed of the river. It had dried up sufficiently for their investigations--in fact, it had dried up more than it had in forty years—so they were able to examine the Taylor Trail rather extensively. After cleaning off the area and mapping it, they made a startling discovery: they found that there were depressions approximating a human print, but at the head of those prints were discolorations--stains or infills. There certainly were discolorations, some of them having depressions--but discolorations are the best way to describe them. They found that there were stains, indicating that a dinosaur had stepped there.

Some of the stains were so clear that they showed in detail the claws of this particular dinosaur in vivid relief. But these were all in stain. Previously the academic evolutionary community had tried to ignore the Paluxy area, but now there were front-page articles, and articles in major journals, accentuating the supposed fact that this trail showed that all this was of dinosaurian origin. Various scholars went to the area-- particularly Dr. John Morris, a very fine scholar who is a creationist--and found that there were indications that a dinosaur had indeed stepped in this trail.

I personally extended the investigation, and spent hundreds of hours at the Taylor site looking through the water, and pumping water out, and in all circumstances. I found that there was evidence that a dinosaur had stepped there. Glen Kuban did some core sampling, and so did John Morris. It was found that there was disturbance underneath those patterns.

I arranged some other experiments. Thus John McKay, an Australian scientist, ran some experiments: he used some particular etchings to see if the stains could be painted on. I ran some experiments in the field, both in and out of the water, with hydrochloric acid. I found there was a very thin veneer of material over the layer, outside the water and under the water, with water covering the tracks more accurately and more rapidly. They were actually showing anything you want in the way of stain: you can write your letters, or even your name-- and you can actually write or etch a dinosaur discoloration.

That verified that the tracks could have been fabricated. However, I have examined them very closely: it is my opinion that they were not fabricated, that they are absolutely genuine, claw stains and all. I have found that the core sampling does indicate disturbance underneath, and probably there is crystallizing of the material underneath the stains, so they are genuine.

I have found that we can watch the stains being reproduced under a very special scenario: it is when a portion of the river is pumped nearly dry and cleaned. When there is a thin layer of water over the track area, the stains begin to show in very clear relief. We followed this with investigation: when it is dry they do not show too well, for they need a thin layer of water over them. We found that ultraviolet radiation penetrates the thin layer of water. In all probability, as the tracks were made in material that had a lot of iron content in the calcium carbonate layer, the crystallization cemented that together and underneath this crystallized area (crystallized because of the weight of the dinosaur) you would have greater iron concentration. By the way, they tend to disappear when the water is deep, and to re-appear when the water is very thin and shallow.

You have an unusual context: the ultraviolet radiation charges the free oxygen in the water, and thus it aggressively forms composite iron oxide Fe_2O_3 and Fe_2O_4, with the iron in the crystallized surface layer.

Don Patton's Important Role ... With Others

So the tracks appear; they are genuine. But then in the summer and early fall of 1988, various researchers went with us to the river, and we were able to pump the river dry. The primary associate in this project was Don Patton, geologist and an outstanding researcher. Jim Freeman and Michael Reddick were the documentarians, and they undertook long and exhaustive hours of work. Tommy Bass also assisted in the project; in addition to that, medical doctor and physiologist Dale Peterson did extensive work with us. There were others as well, but these were the principals involved, all under the direction of the Creation Evidences Museum.

When we pumped the river dry, we found that a dinosaur did step in the Taylor Trail; the trail was originally made by a dinosaur--there was no question about it, but that is not all. We found in every single track of the Taylor Trail--in left-right configuration--a secondary print. There was an eleven and a half-inch print of specific human detail: the heel was there in some respects in some of the prints, and some had all five of the toes, the ball, the flange, the medial arches, and even the lateral arches.

I will now give specific details as to where each of the tracks would be, but first, let me say that on disclosure of these facts, one of our chief critics stated that apparently the dinosaur had an appendage under his foot--a pad that approximated a human foot and thus making both prints simultaneously! We do not name him, only because it is secondhand evidence.

Our critic later hesitated to state that again, but the reporter told us directly that the critic had stated that to her. That really presents a problem as an evolutionary explanation, because these secondary prints--these human configuration prints--are of left-right pace and stride, totally consistent, and they move around within the dinosaur tracks. Let me repeat that: these human- looking tracks are actually located within the dinosaur tracks.

Apparently the individual, this human, had seen that the dinosaur footprints were ahead, with a bit of mud and water having seeped back into the print. You need to realize that anyone walking in uncured calcium carbonate unlithified lime-stone will have his feet burned. It is like walking in uncured concrete. So the individual chose to step within the dinosaur tracks, in all probability to keep his feet washed, and thus relieve the irritation on his feet. This all makes perfect sense when you remember our belief that these were humans seeking higher and higher ground as they sought to escape the rising waters of the flood in Noah's day.

Where Are the Tracks?

Now let me tell you where the tracks are, beginning with Track No. -6:

In Track No. -6 the secondary print is the central rear portion of the dinosaur print.

In Track No. -5 the secondary print is right in

the center of the entire print.

In Track No. -4 the secondary print is to the left center of the dinosaur print.

In Track No. -3C the secondary print is slightly forward in the center.

In Track No. -3B the secondary print is to the left, slightly out of the dinosaur track, but the anterior portion in the center is about forty percent forward in the print; all five toes, ball, flange, metatarsal base, heel, lateral and medial arches, are seen very clearly.

That Fascinating -3B Print

In fact in Dinosaur Track No. -3B the clear print is a tertiary print. In other words, we have a primary print (the dinosaur track), and a secondary print, with the toes extended up under the mud. Then there was a re-adjustment, making the third print (the human print being re-adjusted to make the tertiary print), and that is a perfectly clear print. It is of great interest also to note that the distance between -3B and -3 is only twenty-seven inches. For a person of approximately six feet three inch stature, with a twenty-seven inch adjustment, there would be ample room within the human physiology to stand in the same place and adjust the print as he turned. Thus it would leave a very clear print as the person went forward in Track No. -3.

Incidentally, -7 is a left footprint, -6 is a right, -5 is a left, -4 is a right, -3C is a left, -3B is a right, -3 is a left and it is in a front center portion, -2 is a right and it is the center left portion, while -1 is a left footprint in the center portion of the first dinosaur track. In other words there is clear evidence that this was a trail of human footprints in left-right sequence.

> Track No. +1 is slightly to the right and slightly ahead of center in the dinosaur track.

> Track No. +2 is in the center left, slightly forward.

> Track No. +3 is in the rear of the print, at the absolute center.

> Track No. +4 is in the extreme right forward section--the anterior section of the dinosaur print.

> Track No. +5 is to the left forward center.

> Track No. +6 is to the slight left of the dinosaur print.

All that is the interpretation from the line drawings as done by Don Patton and Jim Collins in consultation with myself as the director of the project. (Further details of this are given in the revised and enlarged edition of *Dinosaur--Scientific Evidence That Dinosaurs and Men Walked Together*.)

So the mystery was solved, but there was a bonus. With us during the research was an anatomist, a medical doctor and physiologist, Dr. Dale Peterson of Oklahoma City. Dr. Peterson is a splendid medical practitioner and scholar. He and I had found the original human print actually in the dinosaur trail; Tommy Bass found the second; we then found a third, and finally we found a fourth print that was five inches in length-- a child's print.

Dr. Peterson then analyzed this extensively, with the great toe, the other toes, the flange area, the semi-flat-footed nature of the print, all being consistent with children's footprints. The heel, the ball and the flange all indicated that it was a genuine human footprint, and the others were also human.

Now the first footprint (that we called the Becky series) was simply stain or discoloration. The position is this: if the dinosaur prints in discoloration and stain are genuine--and scholars do not challenge that--then the human prints in discoloration and stain are also genuine.

In the Ryals case the print is primarily seen by discoloration, and then examination shows all the depressions of a human print around that discoloration.

The Conclusion: Men Walked In Dinosaur Tracks

We are saying that the mystery has been solved. The Taylor Trail is both a dinosaur trail primarily, and a human trail by secondary impressions: there is no question that both were there. Thus the solution to the mystery of the footprints in the Paluxy River and the Paluxy River basin is solved in favor of academic, scientific creationism.

Chapter Seven

Time, Dating Methods, and a Young Earth
by Dr. Carl Baugh

I want to discuss radiometric dating and a young earth. There is a wealth of resource information available which shows that the earth, the solar system, and the entire universe are quite young, calculated within thousands of years. That calculation is not even in tens of thousands, or hundreds of thousands, or millions, and certainly not in billions of years.

Radiometric Dating and a Young Earth
There has been, however, one plaguing problem, and that has been radiometric dating. Various approaches have been given by creation scholars and individuals who have

expertise in a given area, particularly in the area of physics. I certainly do not pose as one having great ability in the area of physics, or unusual disciplinary scholastic research in this area. However, we at the Creation Evidences Museum have formulated a unique orchestral model of creation, and this model--along with relevant published material--certainly answers the primary question of radiometric dating and a young earth. Thus, we want to make a contribution into the field of academic thought, and particularly in the defense of creation as opposed to the evolutionary concept.

As I have mentioned, there is a gold mine of resource material available in the standard literature, and it is available in certain repositories of creationistic thought and disclosure. We will be calling upon some of the accepted authors in this presentation. Then, before the discussion is over, we hope to make a valuable original contribution.

At the Creation Evidences Museum we are assembling data relative to the controversy--a controversy that is not only a modern issue, for it really has been an issue since man was first created. There are four great questions of life, and man always muses over these questions. They are: ''Who am I?'' ''Where did I come from?'' ''What is my purpose here?'' and, ''Where am I going?''

Everyone must grapple with those questions, and in answering them the individual of any culture, civilization, or point in time in history must deal with the evidence he has at hand, and the exposure or revelation of God Himself. We have in the written biblical record the revelation of God Himself, and we have various tangible evidences that would give any thinking individual a clear, calculated, statistical basis for his conviction regarding a literal creation, and a personal Creator.

I want first of all to introduce some material that was compiled by Charles Cooke, then we will go to Chris Pugh, and we will make particular reference to Dr. Robert Gentry's work. This last is an epochal work in the annals of scientific inquiry.

Then we will try to make some original contribution ourselves in the orchestral creation model, as researched at the Creation Evidences Museum.

What Is Radiometric Dating?

There have been long lists of materials regarding radiometric dating that have been published. They are available from such sources as the Institute for Creation Research in San Diego, from Dr. Robert Whitelaw in West Virginia, from the Bible Science Association in Minneapolis, and from the Creation Science Foundation in Brisbane, Australia. The published material available from these sources gives a very strong academic basis for scientific creation.

Let us begin with this consideration: What is radiometric dating?

There are certain elements that are unstable, some over a short range, some over a long range. These elements actually give off an alpha particle--or radiate energy, essentially--and this has resulted in some tremendous strides being made in the area of physics. That is so in reference to the atomic and hydrogen bombs, in reference to nuclear power plants, in reference to many power systems which have powered our instruments on the moon and in space flight. So there certainly has been an analog of actual contribution that is beneficial, non-detrimental, and non-warlike. These contributions have certainly encouraged research which, if taken at face value, points to creation--and to a recent creation at that.

In our consideration of recency we will deal particularly with a unique contribution made at the Creation Evidences Museum in this field. The radiometric concept simply means that the element radiates energy: as it does naturally, it then goes to another state in its nucleus. This is called transmutation. It is transmuted from being one element, and then it has a daughter product, a by-product. Thus the concept relates to the amount of time that it takes for a particular element which is radioactive to give off energy in the form of an alpha particle, etc. As it gives off this energy and a bit of its nucleus, it is radioactive. Some elements are rather stable, and some are less stable.

The half-life of a radioactive material is simply the calculation showing the amount of time on average that it takes this material to lose half its mass as it naturally radiates its energy and particles from the nucleus, thus transmuting itself into another element.

To give you an idea regarding the half-life, we will introduce the concept by giving a general background of evidence. This supports the fact that there are many indications to show that the earth is extremely young, measured in only thousands of years.

For instance, Layelle, who a little over a century ago was a publicist in trying to show that the earth's system proved an evolutionary time scale, set a false reference for the decay of Niagara Falls. He claimed that as the water of the fall proceeds over the stone layer, it cuts away at the basic material. He gave this false record, arguing that it would have taken at least thirty-five thousand years for Niagara Falls to have been formed--considering that it would have begun at the very edge of the entire precipice, the tectonic layering of the stone material. However, what he gave was a false readout and that has been corrected. The readout shows that it would not have taken thirty-five thousand years for the formation of the Niagara Falls but --depending on various concepts--it would take something between four thousand and nine thousand years to produce the falls as we know them today.

Bias and Error

So in our consideration of this particular subject of recency we must be aware that individuals have approached the concept with a bias, and have even publicized material which is in error. Let me give a listing of indicators of recency:

First of all, ancient written records indicate recency. *Robert Young's Concordance* (in its twenty-second edition) lists thirty-seven ancient written records, all of which place the date of Creation no earlier than 7000 B.C., and many of them much more recent than that. I am using the list that Charles Cooke has compiled relating to recency, because that is the one I have on hand at the moment. Others are available.

The second indicator that Charles Cooke gives is the Nile River overflow. A measurement of the sediment of the Nile River's flooding each year gives a maximum age of less than thirty thousand years...let us remember that: thirty thousand years is a *maximum* age. He further points out that if we consider a couple of major deposition times, that brings the measurements all within the time of the biblical record. And certainly there are flooding times which are far beyond the normal, and beyond the average. Therefore this can indeed be calculated within biblical times, and within the time that we normally assign to the Noahic flood.

The third area listed is salt in the sea. The amount of sodium chloride (the common table salt in the oceans and the Dead Sea) gives the age of the earth as being under thirteen thousand years. Measuring uranium salt instead of sodium chloride, we have a figure of less than ten thousand years, and that certainly would be within the biblical framework. We are not arguing for or against dates such as Bishop Ussher's 4004 B.B. for creation. We are simply making the point that only a few thousand years are involved.

Fourthly, the cooling of the earth: Lord Kelvin's calculations of the rate of heat flow through the surface of the earth demolished Lyall's uniformitarian assumption, making the time too short for evolution--and those are standard calculations of which we should be well aware.

Fifth, Cooke mentions oil geysers. Studies of the

permeability of the rocks surrounding oil beds show that any pressure build-up would be dissipated and bled off the surrounding rocks within a few thousand years. Yet there is enough pressure within oil wells to produce a tremendous geyser when the well is struck, so therefore we have tangible geologic information showing that it all had to be recent.

The sixth area that he points to is carbon-14 disintegration. Calculations show that the carbon-14 clock should have begun about eight thousand years ago or less. There are many areas (and that is not the major area of our present consideration) which show that when carbon-14 is re-assigned, the evidence points to within the last few thousand years as a reference guide. The work of Dr. Robert Whitelaw is highly relevant in this area.

Seventh, ocean sediment is listed. There are about twenty-eight billion tons of sediment added to the oceans each year. The layer of sediment on the bottom of the ocean's floor would be one hundred miles thick if the earth was old enough to allow for evolutionary time, and of course it is absolutely impossible for it to be one hundred miles thick--it is certainly *not* like that. The sediments are rather thin in many areas, indicating just a few thousand years of sedimentary deposit on the floors of the oceans.

Eighth, the influx of cosmic dust: if the earth and the moon had been here for billions of years, there should be fifty or more feet of dust on the earth's surface. In fact, calculations show that it would range from fifty to nine hundred and fifty feet of dust on the moon and dust on the earth. So, since that is not the case, and since the moon dust averages only a fraction of an inch, this would indicate only thousands of years--just a few thousand years rather than the millions or billions of years that are suggested by standard cosmology. (Cosmology deals with evolutionary considerations of how things began, and how they have continued over long periods of time.)

Ninth, the decay of comets: the fact that comets still have

tails and mass (though many have appeared and re-appeared in the visual sky), suggests that the solar system is young.

Tenth: a major area of consideration of which the standard evolutionist is normally not aware, is the area of population statistics. Let us pause for a moment and consider this. If there are no gaps in the genealogical lists of early Genesis, the flood could have been as recent as 4300 B.P. ("before present"). If we accept that date for the purpose of this exercise, the population today is certainly within the framework of statistical analysis. The population today is what the standard population equation would predict--let me repeat that: the population we observe today is what the standard population equation would predict.

Let me go into some detail on this. The recent world population growth rate is calculated at just under two percent per year. Let us be conservative in our consideration and consider what the average individual would say: "If you are going to simply take 4300 B.P. for the time of the flood, only eight souls were there. There were four families, but only three with population-bearing abilities--the three sons of Noah and their wives. So there just is not enough time to produce the five billion people we have on the face of the earth today."

Let us look at the statistics, and we shall be conservative in our approach. I have already said that the recent world population growth rate has been calculated at just under two percent--but let us consider it as being only one percent. Let us also calculate into this equation the fact that wars and diseases and plagues have certainly played a large part in population statistics. So let us allow for this, and let us be very generous and assume that a third of the population existing at any time on the face of the globe would be wiped out every eighty-two years. There is a standard reason and a solid basis for this consideration of eighty-two years.

Now, using 4300 B.P. for the minimum date for the flood, at the conservative one percent growth rate figure with frequent population decimations because of disease, war, famine, plagues, etc., in forty-three hundred years we would produce just under four and a half billion people--and that is using a one percent growth rate! If we elevate that to the standard, to the current two percent growth rate, we certainly would have no difficulty producing all the people on the face of the globe today--but even at the conservative figure of one percent growth rate we can produce them.

Now here is the real problem for the evolutionary concept. According to the theory of evolution, at least one to three and a half million years have gone by since the dawn of the first couple, when the first man and woman arrived on the face of the globe. Even if we used the same conservative values as we have above, we find that long age evolution hits what some scholars have called a brick wall. Using the standard figures and decimating the earth with one third of the population removed every eighty-two years, the population after only forty-one thousand years would be 2×10^{89}--and that is incredible. If you have spent much time in consideration of values and physics, you know that the estimated number of electrons available in the entire universe is under 10^{85}.

What this really means is that there would not be enough space in the entire universe to hold the people that would have been born and supposedly still existing on Planet Earth today. Can you imagine what it would be after a million years? We are only considering forty-one thousand years, so what we are saying is that there is tangible academic scientific evidence in support of recency, and concurrently with that there is evidence in contradiction of long age.

The Missing Radiogenic Helium

Number 11 as listed in this chart of Charles Cooke is the missing radiogenic helium. We have uranium-238 losing its mass, and in its decay it gives off an alpha particle. This particular alpha particle is unique: because of its total charge of uniqueness it recombines with other particles to form helium-4. A standard helium atom is helium-3, and our statisticians are able to give a very clear indication as to how much helium-3 there is in the atmosphere, and in the available surface material of the globe. At the same time they are able to calculate the amount of helium-4, and even if all the helium-4 had been produced by the decay of uranium, this comes out to involve less than fifteen thousand years of time.

Taking it more conservatively, it is calculated to be a little over six thousand years of time that has passed--and that is considering that all of the helium-4 had been made by the decay of uranium, not considering any helium-4 having been here in origin. So when we take the actual statistics it is impossible for us to have long ages.

Number 12 listed is stalactites and stalagmites. The reasonable age for the formation of stalactites and stalagmites in limestone cavern formations is less than five thousand years. Actually in the base of the Lincoln Monument in Washington, D.C. we have entire columns of this material--produced in little over one hundred years of time. So when you are given the long tens of millions of years for stalactites and stalagmites by lecturers in cavern context, that is in absolute error.

The Earth's Decaying Magnetic Field

Number 13 is the earth's decaying magnetic field. An outstanding physicist, Dr. Thomas Barnes, has done unique work and made a major contribution in the field of scientific inquiry relative to the decay of the earth's magnetic field. It has been found that every fourteen hundred years the earth loses half its energy in its magnetic field. That means that fourteen hundred years ago the earth's magnetic field would have been twice what it is today; fourteen hundred years before that it would have had four times what it is today; fourteen hundred years before that, eight times what it is today!

On this basis if you go back anything approaching ten thousand years in a time period, you get into major difficulties. If you extrapolate back fifteen thousand years in time, the situation becomes impossible. Anything approaching that time would indicate that the magnetic field of the earth would have the value or strength of a magnetic star.

This is a major problem for the evolutionary concept. Consequently it is normally suggested, ''Well, the magnetic field of the earth reverses itself.'' That is not necessarily so; but in any case the indications of the reversal, even if it did reverse itself, are that it would not lose its strength in that reversal.

There is no dynamic context to generate such a mobile formation. In addition, lightning strikes and discharge of energy can also charge the miniscule rock layers and give the same results as if the earth's magnetic field had reversed itself.

So there is no convincing indication that the field has reversed itself, and even if there were, it would not have lost its energy. So it is a major problem for those who consider long periods of time to be in evidence.

The Decrease of the Sun's Diameter

Number 14 is the decrease in the sun's diameter. A few years ago it was announced that the sun was shrinking at such a rate that the major astrophysicists would have to interpret all of this in a biblical context of a few thousand years. However, scurrying to the rescue, some astrophysicists examined various possibilities and said, ''Well, that was just a major influx; it will average out over a period of time.''

Even if that were the case, and even if we had only a small amount of surface diameter lost each century, we still have the same major problem going back into tens of thousands of years.

In any case, even if the sun is not losing surface mass,

it is losing energy, and ultimately we will have the same result. Therefore if we extrapolate back something like one hundred thousand years in the past, the discharge of mass and energy of the sun in bathing us with the particles necessary for the synthesis of life forms would have been so great that the earth would have simply been swallowed in the process. Since the earth has not been so swallowed, if we are to be logical in all this, we must simply deduce that the earth--and the sun--are quite young.

Atomic Clocks and the Earth's Spin Rate

Number 15 is the earth's spin rate. Atomic clocks which have measured for many years the earth's spin rate to the merest billionth of a second, have consistently found that the earth is slowing down at the rate of one second a year. If the earth were billions of years old, its initial spin rate would have been so great that centrifugal force would have greatly deformed the earth, and we do not see that as being the case. Therefore, losing a second per year would indicate that we simply do have thousands--and not millions--of years in the calculation.

As a matter of fact, the calculations are even more for a "young earth" for another reason. If in earlier times the earth was spinning faster--and that is established--it means it was also slowing down faster and so in those times it would have been losing more than a second a year. This means that the concept of it being young is even more definite than with the present rate of slowing down, which is about a second a year.

These various considerations have been given for a number of years and the evolutionary community has simply said essentially, "We know those are problems, but we have a major argument in favor of long age, and this the radiometric decay rate."

That is really what we want to address in an abbreviated

form in this particular discussion. I should mention that various elements such as uranium, polonium, rubidium, strontium, thorium, potassium, etc. can be produced in the laboratory but they are also found in nature--and they lose their mass in a process of radiation. As they lose that mass, there is a standard calculation at the point from which half of the original material is still left--and it is all still in the process of decaying. That being the case, we would be aware of the fact that a stable isotope (radioactive material which is stable and takes some period of time to decay) can be defined as one having a half-life greater than 10^{18} of years--these are in standard calculations.

Remember, the times we are giving are taken from recognized tables--we do *not* endorse them as fact. Nevertheless here is the argument: Uranium 238, the heaviest natural particle or natural element, normally decays into lead-206 with a half-life of 4.51 billion years. Uranium-235 normally decays into lead-207 with a half- life of 710 million years. Thorium-232 normally decays into lead-208 with a half-life of 14.1 billion years. This just gives you an indication of these supposed time periods.

However, it has been embarrassing to certain evolutionary scholars to find that in the laboratory those involved in this discipline have been able to produce synthetic or man-made isotopes which are not found in nature, and which have been found to be stable. These are radioactive materials and they have been produced in the laboratory. Yet in that point in time, and by production in the laboratory, these particular elements have half-lives which indicate that they are billions of years old--yet they were made in the laboratory by synthetic man-made methods.

I will give an abbreviated synopsis of them by their technical and scientific classification: Pb_{205}, which has a half-life of 1.43×10^7 of years; Pu_{244} has a half-life of 8.26×10 years; and Cm_{247} has a half- life of 1.56×10^7 of years.

These long-life radio-isotopes were first created by

man in the laboratory. They already had the appearance of having been there for millions or even billions of years--that is, if we use the standard interpretation that the half-life indicates how long they have been around.

The simple fact is that the half-life does not indicate how long they have been around, but it may indicate both their youthfulness and their usefulness.

Dr. Robert Gentry's Sensational Work

Now we come to the introduction of a major scholar, Dr. Robert Gentry. Dr. Gentry has made a major contribution in the field of scientific inquiry as well as scientific creationism. He has carried on the research of halos, and these halos are a major point for consideration.

The particular radioactive halos that have been prominent in his inquiry are pleochroic halos. These are tiny little concentric rings which are formed as radioactive material decays, and it decays with a particular level of energy. Therefore it makes a consistent signature. The signature of radioactive materials is more accurate than your thumb print, and these radioactive signatures have been left in the granite of the earth-- the crystalline material of the earth. They have been left in chain reaction context--that is, you have a parent/daughter, parent/ daughter relationship, one transmuting into another element, into another, and into another, and the signature is left there showing that transmutation line. This can be duplicated in the laboratory, from one element into another. The radioactive decay rate can be measured with absolute precision: it is in the written record of the granite.

However, something else has been startling to the academic community. Not only do you find in this biotite-- micrographite, etc.--crystalline materials in the granite (Dr. Gentry and others have found the chain reaction)--but you find also evidence of additional radioactive signature--pleochroic halo signature. These are tiny little rings of energy signature that were left when the entire additional process was going on, but it was not a part of the chain. In the chain you have the same elements, but over on the side in independent signature display you have the same materials. In these materials found over on the side is the signature left by polonium-218 which has a half-life of 3.05 minutes, meaning that essentially in a matter of minutes it is all gone.

What that would say is that the entire context of the granite structure had to be created intact within a given day-- literally within minutes!

But there is something even more staggering. Dr. Gentry and others found over on the side another part of the chain reaction in this particular consideration, polonium-214. The half-life of polonium-214 is .000164 seconds, meaning that essentially in less than a fraction of a second it would all be gone; so, essentially faster than we can snap our fingers, the granite would have been created with the radioactive materials in place and operational.

This would indicate not only a younger, but an instantaneous creation to that earth. And we want to take the academic facts at face value: take them simply for what they are. That would indicate that not only within a particular day of time was this done but, as Dr. Gentry points out, in Psalm 33 we read, *"The Lord of the heavens spake and it was done."* It stood fast just by the spoken word; with the time required to say it, it was done. So this would indicate immediacy. In Genesis 1, we read that *"God said, let there be...."* His word meant instantaneous creation.

Now let us of the Creation Evidences Museum make a contribution to this field of inquiry. I will simply outline some of the considerations given in my book, *Panorama of Creation*. The orchestral creation model is the basis for this model which has been researched at the Creation Evidences Museum. We are not indicating that all the material has been original, or that all the research has been original. It certainly has not been: we have had to lean on the research of outstanding scholars who over decades and even centuries have done splendid work in their areas. Nevertheless the compilation of this orchestral model has been the result of the work of researchers associated with the Creation Evidences Museum, and certain areas of it have been original work. The following is one such area.

Go Back ... to Less and Less Chaos

When we consider that the radioactive elements are not natural to the surface and atmosphere, let us put them back to where evidence shows they came from. Those on the surface and those in sedimentary rocks, and in certain igneous rocks, have obviously come from inside the earth. They have been expunged from inside the earth, and in our model this expunging primarily took place in the first few days, and weeks, and months of the worldwide flood of Noah's day.

So let us put them back inside the earth. Now let us go beyond that; let the earth itself be our guide. In stable position we find radioactive materials in the granite. The granite is certainly the crust, the foundation of the surface of the earth, and when we find these materials in the granite they are distributed so perfectly that the granite does not explode. If they were not distributed so well we would actually have a chain nuclear reaction set off in the granite itself. We do not have that occurring, so the distribution is in foundations within the granite. The distribution is a line so perfectly set that we do not have a chain reaction nuclear explosion or a meltdown occurring in the granite. It's amazing, isn't it? What plan and control there is behind all creation!

So let what is found in the earth naturally be our guide. Let us put the radioactive elements back inside the earth, and let us put them in the natural context found in the granite. That would indicate a system of perfect balance and layering inside the earth, or in foundations inside the earth.

It is gratifying to find in Job 38 the Creator speaking to man, to Job in particular. It is as if man--in the person of Job-- had been there when He, the Creator God, actually placed the foundations in their alignments.

Of course, man was not really there. This occurred apparently on Day Three of the creation week. So let us put them back in foundation alignment, in perfect alignment. What do we get? When radioactive materials are aligned and distributed with design we get controlled heat, and I should say as a spin-off process if the design were appropriate, we could get a breeder reaction so that we would end up with additional fissionable material.

What we have here is a system of the granite encasing foundations which feather out all the way to the core of the earth, but these would not be in their molten context as we find them writhing within the heart of the earth today. They would have been in perfect balance, because--given enough time back in the past--that writhing, voluptuous context found within the crust of the earth would certainly have originated with control and balance. That is simply due to the second law of thermodynamics, the law of entropy: if the current chaos is extrapolated back in time, there is less and less chaos, until you go back far enough in time and you have perfect balance.

So let us put it back in perfect balance. This would indicate a gentle radiation of heat, a controlled radiation of heat: thermal exchange. Also, within the earth there are great reservoirs of water: let us place these waters back in time in conjunction with moderating elements which are in conjunction with perfectly balanced and distributed radioactive elements. Then we simply have the waters within the earth gently heated, and this heat being radiated out to the surface of the earth. In the orchestral creation model this is not only quite advantageous, but it is necessary.

In Times Past There Was a Canopy

There is academic evidence to support the position that at some time in the past there was a canopy, a firmament over the earth giving greater atmospheric pressure. This permitted the flying Pterosaurs to proliferate and to soar in the skies. Simultaneously, this permitted the dinosaurs, which have a small lung capacity, to enjoy life on Planet Earth, because under two atmospheres of pressure, with slightly enriched oxygen, the entire blood plasma becomes saturated with oxygen. That being the case, then the great dinosaurs with small lung capacities could essentially have a field day. The fact that they lived and proliferated on every continent of the globe, even north of the Arctic Circle, and in the Antarctic as well, indicates that we had such a firmament.

In the biblical record at Genesis 1:6, that firmament is stated as having originated at the creation by God Himself on Day Two. That firmament, that canopy, would have had to be extremely frigid in order to remain in place.

This means that, due to its frigid nature and due to the fact that it was composed of the elements of water, the shortwave radiation from the sun and solar cosmic radiation would have been filtered out. This would have given a superior context. It also would have filtered out not only the shortwave radiation which is partially contributing to the energy level and heat build-up during the day on Planet Earth, but it would have filtered to some degree the infrared, which certainly adds to the heat build-up on Planet Earth. This means you would only have a moderate build-up of heat during the day on Planet Earth under such a canopy. This further means that you would need an additional moderating thermal factor.

In other words, you would need the furnace in the basement, with the beautiful orchestrated design of these radioactive materials within the earth simply doing their thing. That is to say, they would be giving off thermal exchange heat as they radiated. It would certainly appear that they were part of the design factor in our beautifully designed earth, and that would mean over billions and billions of years and then--considering the breeder reactor context--essentially for an eternity. This physical Planet Earth would be sustained if all of these radioactive elements were in perfect balance, created and orchestrated. That is simply the way our Creator does things.

A Personal, Caring, All-Powerful Creator

The contribution that we have made into this field of radiometric dating and a young earth is to simply state that the radioactive decay rate does not show that these elements have been around for millions or billions of years. It shows that they were designed, orchestrated, and created instantly in place, with a purpose of radiating at various rates and levels in order to maintain the thermal temperatures necessary for life to be carried on on Planet Earth. Thus the entire model is orchestrated--and that by a personal, caring, all-powerful Creator.

Chapter Eight
The Seedplot of the Bible
by Dr. Clifford Wilson

(Reproduced with permission from *The Early Chapters of Genesis* by Dr. Clifford Wilson.)

Great Doctrines About God

Genesis Chapters 1 through 11 have rightly been called the "seedplot of the Bible." In that remarkable introductory section of God's Word there are essential points of doctrine and of history.

We shall briefly outline some of the major doctrines about God that are contained therein. First we recognize that God is the great Creator, with the very first verse stating, *"In the beginning God created the heaven and the earth."* The actual words in Hebrew are *bara Elohim* (the verb comes first)--"the Gods, He created." This is sometimes called the Hebrew royal plural, but implicitly it is far more than just a particular linguistic form. Implicit in that statement *bara Elohim* is the concept of the Godhead, plural, being one in purpose and action, for the verb *bara* is the singular form of "created." It is "the Gods, He created." It is sometimes said that in the Old the New is concealed, and in the New the Old is revealed. The doctrine of the Trinity, the Triune God, is not brought out into the open in the Old Testament, but it was there implicitly. In the New Testament the doctrine is stated explicitly, as in the formula for baptism--baptizing them in the name of the Father, and of the Son, and of the Holy Spirit.

So at the very beginning of Genesis we read that God is in fact the Godhead, acting as One, while the New Testament makes it clear that the Father, the Son, and the Holy Spirit were all involved in this great process of creation. And in the New Testament we learn that by Him, Jesus, all things were created (Col. 1:16), for His pleasure (Rev. 4:11).

God Is the Great Revealer

Then we read in this "seedplot of the Bible" that God is the great Revealer. We have good reason to believe that the early chapters of Genesis were actually written on clay tablets. There is what is called a "colophon" between the various tablets. That is to be found at those points where we read, "These are the generations of...." It is as though we are looking at a series of family tablets, with one person telling the family story, and then another member taking it up. It is interesting to find that the record recommences at a time when an important figure whose record is in the preceding section has just died. It is almost as though there is a funeral service, and tablets relating to the family tree are handed on. The story continues, apparently written down on clay tablets.

That concept of the colophon is known in ancient literature, and was especially developed by P.J. Wiseman in his book, *New Discoveries in Babylonia About Genesis*, written in 1948. In later years his son, D.J. Wiseman, was professor of Assyriology at the London University in England. He brought out another book, *Clues to Creation in Genesis*, dealing with the early chapters of Genesis, and updating his father's writings. (His father had been killed in an air crash in the late 1940s.) Professor Wiseman endorsed the basic principles of what his father had earlier written.

It is interesting to notice that part of the famous Epic of Gilgamesh was found at Megiddo in northern Israel, dating to about the time of the Conquest. It seems that somebody had taken that tablet across the Fertile Crescent, up between the Rivers Euphrates and Tigris from somewhere in ancient Babylonia, right over into Israel. If that could happen with a well-known document such as the Epic of Gilgamesh, it could also happen with these early records of Genesis. It seems that Abraham was not born first, but became the ''priest'' of his family, apparently having the rights of the firstborn (shown by comparison of the ages given in relation to Terah and his sons in Genesis 11 and in the speech of Stephen at Acts 7). As the priestly firstborn, certain rights would accrue to Abraham, possibly including the ownership of these important ancestral tablets. It is quite likely that he had them in his possession, took them with him into Israel, and that centuries later they came into the possession of the leader Moses who then edited them into the form of the book we now call Genesis.

Moses was not there at the time that the Genesis records were written--Abraham lived some hundreds of years before the time of Moses, and of course the great men of faith in the early chapters of Genesis were many hundreds of years before Moses, and even well before Abraham.

Where did the knowledge come from for the first tablet? The answer is, from God. It seems that He revealed the intimate details about creation to Adam, the first man. Adam could not have known them, for the marvelous record of the first five days of creation took place before he himself was brought into being. And so as we continue the concept of doctrines in the early chapters of Genesis, we see that God Himself is the great Revealer. That teaching is continued in the New Testament, where we read that the Lord Jesus Christ is made unto us wisdom and righteousness--He Himself is the very Word of God, the One Who reveals God to us.

Then we find a third concept--that God is not only Creator and Revealer, but He is also the Friend of man. The Godhead said, *"Let us make man in our image"*--and man was made to be a friend of God. God would walk with Adam in the Garden of Eden, and would converse with him. Man was made to be His friend. Abraham would later be referred to as the friend of God and, despite his failings, David was referred to as someone "after the heart of God." Man and woman were made to be God's friends. We read in Genesis 1:27, *"So God created man in his own image, in the image of God created he him; male and female created he them."* The concept of man includes woman. Perhaps the term "mankind" would make the concept clearer today.

However, although man was created to be the friend of God, it is also true that God is a holy God and certain standards were expected of man. Man was given a condition that he must not eat of the Tree of the Knowledge of Good and Evil in the Garden. However, he did so, and as a result he necessarily knew the judgment of God. God is therefore seen as the Judge. When His standards are put aside, He must come in judgment. Thus in Genesis 3 we have the story of the fall, of God's judgment, and of man being put out from the Garden of Eden. God was necessarily the Judge. The concept of judgment is shown throughout Scripture, not only at the time of the fall of man, but again when man became so totally evil that God decreed his destruction. Only Noah and his family were saved in the ark that God told Noah to prepare. At Calvary, the Lord Jesus Christ took to Himself the judgment of God, as He who knew no sin became sin for us. He was judged because He took the place of me, the sinner. The concept of judgment is there through all the New Testament but, thank God, the judgment is borne by another, and you and I can go free if we accept Him as our Substitute.

The Revealer, Friend and Judge Is Also the Redeemer

That leads to a fifth concept, for this One who is Creator, Revealer, Friend and Judge, is also the Redeemer. Redemption has the idea of buying back, especially out of slavery. Throughout the Scriptures we find that the fact of buying back is a very real concept. When we come to the New Testament we find that we were as slaves in a marketplace, but the Lord Jesus Christ has come to redeem us, to buy us back. He paid for that which was already His own, and the price He paid was the full price. He paid with His blood--His life. He gave His life for the redemption of mankind--slaves to sin. And because He is eternal, His death can cover the death of every individual who will put his trust in the Lord Jesus Christ. He is the Redeemer--the Kinsman-Redeemer--the One who said, ''Here am I, send Me.'' Because He died, I am redeemed, purchased in the marketplace, and no longer a slave to sin.

God Is the Restorer

Then there is a sixth concept, for not only is He the Redeemer, but He is also the Restorer. It is not enough to know that we have been bought out of the marketplace, because we need also to have our condition reversed. We are brought back into a Garden of Eden situation. In the epistle to the Ephesians, we read that we are seated with Christ in the heavenly places-- no longer slaves, but sitting as heirs of God, joint-heirs with Jesus Christ. We are redeemed, and we are restored. When the Lord Jesus Christ restored that which He did not take away, we were brought back into a living relationship with the great

Creator who is also our Saviour, our Friend, our Redeemer, and our Restorer.

Finally--although no doubt other doctrines are to be found within these chapters--this portion of Scripture introduces us to the concept that God is the God of the covenant. Certain promises were made to Adam and Eve, but they were conditional. Man must not eat of the fruit of the Tree of Knowledge of Good and Evil, and when he did so it was necessary for God to put him forth from the Garden of Eden. Otherwise they might have eaten of the Tree of Life that was right there in the center of the Garden. That would have been tragic indeed, for it would have meant that man would have lived forever, but with the ever-increasing agonies associated with his fallen state. He would eventually take to his body all the illnesses, diseases, and infections that have ever been known to man: leprosy, cancer, and so much more. He would have had a body that would never die, and that would ultimately endure the agonies of hell within that body. In His love God put forth the man from the Garden, but provided a way in that as soon as the judgment was declared, so also was the promise of the Redeemer.

This God is the great covenant-keeping God, and we are reminded of that again in the covenant that was entered into with Abraham. At John 8:58 we read of the Lord Jesus Christ saying *"Before Abraham was, I Am."* He also told the Jewish leaders that Abraham rejoiced to see His day, and he saw it and was glad. Probably that referred to the time when the Lord Jesus Christ in a Christophany, as the angel of the Lord, appeared to Abraham when Abraham was in the Plain of Mamre just before the cities of Sodom and Gomorrah were destroyed. God entered into a covenant with Abraham, and in doing so the Lord Jesus Christ was, of course, ultimately totally involved. As we have said, it was He who ultimately sealed that covenant with His own blood.

Now a new covenant has been entered into, a covenant

that is unconditional, and is totally efficacious because the Lord Jesus Christ is the sin-bearer who has put away sin by the sacrifice of Himself. He the sinless one could take the full penalty of our sins, past, present, and future, and our covenant-keeping God has entered into a new relationship with us. The prophet Jeremiah said that a new covenant would be given, a new covenant that was fulfilled with the death of the covenant-maker--the Lord Jesus Christ Himself. Now there is a new covenant, a new testament, because we are sealed by the blood of Christ in an eternal relationship of oneness with God. The covenant-keeping God has pledged Himself as our security.

Christ Is the Creator Who Sustains

So in these early chapters of Genesis we see that Christ is the Creator who sustains. The Holy God is the God who judges; Christ is the Redeemer who restores. We also see that man is failing in time but we are pointed on to the unfailing Man in eternity, even the Son of God Himself. In these chapters we see the grief of God, and we look on to the Lord Jesus Christ who said, *"If it be possible, let this cup pass from me, nevertheless, not my will, but thine be done"*--in the Garden of Gethsemane--so different from that other scene with another man (Adam) in another garden (Eden). Christ has been made unto us redemption and righteousness.

And so Genesis chapters 1 through 11 are the ''seedplot of the Bible'' in relation to doctrine.

The Seedplot of the Bible as to History

We also find that early chapters of Genesis are the ''seedplot of the Bible'' as regards history. The more we study the Bible in relation to archaeology, the more we are impressed with the fact that the Bible is meant to be taken seriously as a record of history. In fact, it is the most accurate history text the world has ever known. That can be demonstrated by many confirmations of Bible history, shown from the work of modern archaeologists. At times it has seemed that archaeology has contradicted the Bible, but invariably when the facts are properly established it is the Bible that is shown to be right after all.

Many times even some of the great scholars of archaeology have had to revise their point of view. I was an area supervisor at the excavation of Gezer in Israel back in 1969. At that time I heard a wonderful lecture from the late Professor Nelson Glueck, and among other things he stated, ''I have excavated for thirty years with the Bible in one hand and a trowel in the other. In matters of historical perspective I have never yet found the Bible to be in error.'' Professor Glueck was a Jewish rabbi, and he was not necessarily endorsing all that the so-called fundamentalist Christians would claim for Genesis chapters 1 through 11. He was referring specifically to established historical records, but his point is very important.

Over and over again scholars have had to come back to the fact that if the Bible records make statements about history, it is wise to take those statements at face value. We read at Psalm 119:89, *''For ever, O Lord, thy word is settled in heaven.''* It almost seems that God deliberately takes those areas where criticisms have been leveled against the Scriptures and shows that the scholars who opposed the record were wrong.

Prophecies Against Known Backgrounds

That applies to criticisms of the writings of Moses, and especially the so-called documentary hypothesis which claimed that the Old Testament records of Abraham, and even Moses, were campfire stories which grew in the telling, ultimately put into writing well after the times of Solomon. The critics have been shown to be wrong.

It is true also with the writings about David--critics said that the Psalms of David should be dated to the Maccabean period, eight hundred years after the times of David. Then came the findings of Ram Shamra (the ancient Ugarit) on the Mediterranean sea coast of Syria. Soon scholars saw the relevance of recovered documents to the Psalms of David. The great archaeologist, Professor William Foxwell Albright-- arguably the greatest archaeologist the world has ever seen-- eventually wrote that to suggest that the Psalms of David should be dated to the Maccabean period is absurd (his word). David's prophetic Psalms (such as Psalm 22 about Christ's crucifixion) were genuinely put in writing one thousand years before the event.

The same goes for the New Testament writings. Critics a century ago claimed that some New Testament documents were basically pseudepigraphic (written by someone else), and should be dated to one or even two centuries after the time of Christ. Then came the findings at the Fayum region in Egypt about the turn of the twentieth century. Excavators such as Professors Grenfell, Hunt, and Hogarth came across massive amounts of papyrus documents which eventually made it clear that the New Testament writings were in *koine* Greek, the everyday language of New Testament times. Massive amounts of papyrus documents were put inside sacred crocodiles as part of their embalming processes. A tremendous amount of light has been thrown on the New Testament records, and as a result the New Testament has been endorsed in ways that are quite remarkable. These and other great findings from the libraries of ancient times have done much to dramatically restore the credibility of the Bible writers at points where critics had said that the Bible was wrong.

One important conclusion in relatively modern times is that the records of Genesis chapters 1 through 11 were also meant to be taken as literal history. That has been especially endorsed since the translation of fragments of the Epic of

Atrahasis, and archaeologists have had to recognize that this document contained fragments of such important historical records as creation and the flood in the one on-going document. It becomes clear by comparison that the Bible writers regarded the early chapters of Genesis also as an actual historical record. There are interesting comparisons and contrasts between the records of Genesis and tablets recovered from archaeology. The Bible writings are consistently superior.

In the outline that follows we briefly summarize some of the ways in which the recovered documents from ancient civilizations touch the Bible records. We consistently find that the Bible records must be taken seriously, as actual historical documents and not merely as legends or folklore.

We have said that Genesis chapters 1 through 11 have been called the "seedplot of the Bible," telling us great truths about God who is Creator, Judge, Redeemer, the One who would be the Friend of man, and would walk with him--as in the case of Enoch (Gen. 5:24). We have also seen that these chapters are a bird's-eye view of history, giving us an essential background to the great figure of Abraham, who then emerges and becomes the founder of the Hebrew nation.

History Starts with Genesis Chapter 1: A Survey

We stated that history starts with Genesis chapter 1, where the majestic story of the creation of the heaven and the earth is given. We are immediately challenged to a step of faith, for the Bible does not argue about the existence of God: that noble yet simple statement is the Divine declaration, to be accepted by faith: *"In the beginning God created the heaven and the earth."*

To put these chapters in perspective, the following summary is included.

Genesis chapter 1, which is the record of creation, has surface similarities to the Babylonian epic, *Enuma Elish*. However, the Babylonian epic has been corrupted and distorted through the centuries, and it contains grotesque absurdities. The *Epic of Atrahasis* refers to creation and the flood, and scholars believe it points to an actual historical record (which Genesis is). Tablets from Ebla in Syria (recovered in the 1970s and many of them dating to about 2300 B.C.) make reference to one great being who had formed the earth and the heavens, the sun and the moon. This answered the earlier criticism that such concepts were too early for Moses.

Genesis chapter 2, telling about the Garden of Eden, has some similarity to the *Epic of Emmerkar*. It refers to the Land of Dilmun, ''a clean and bright place where the lion does not kill, the wolf does not snatch the lamb.'' The Ebla tablets included Dilmun in a list of actual places.

Genesis chapter 3 records the fall of man. There are surface similarities in the Babylonian *Myth of Adapa*, such as the ''food of life'' being similar to the ''Tree of Life,'' but the origin of human sin is not envisaged. Scheming, immoral gods were obviously not involved in the creation of a perfectly moral man. Seals depicting a man, a woman, and a serpent have been found at Tepe Gawra, north of Nineveh, and at Nineveh itself--the latter showing a tree also. They might point back to the fall.

Genesis chapter 4 tells of Cain building a city (vs. 17). Verse 21 speaks of harps and organs, and verse 22 points to the early use of metal. Despite earlier beliefs to the contrary, excavations endorse the general picture of this chapter, as at Tell Hassuna, Nineveh, Tell Chagar Bazar, and other sites.

Genesis chapter 5 records details of men who lived for hundreds of years. The effects of sin and disease were not as great then as now. Climate and atmospheric conditions were probably dramatically different before the flood. This is hinted at in the *Sumerian King List*, found at ancient Kish. It tells of kings *before the flood* who lived for thousands of years. Those *after the flood* lived for very much shorter periods. Recent research suggests that the Babylonian figures can be translated differently, to give figures similar to those in Genesis. (This involves using a system based on sixes rather than decimals.)

Genesis chapters 6 through 9 record the events immediately preceding the flood, the flood itself, and the after-events. Finds such as those at Ur, Kish, and Fara indicate floods at different times--*not* the biblical flood, for God said it would not be repeated (Gen. 9:11). The Bible tells of a holy God who decreed judgment on sinful man. There is nothing grotesque or absurd, as there is in the Babylonian *Epic of Gilgamesh* (with Tablet No. 11 telling about the flood).

Genesis chapter 10 contains the remarkable "Table of Nations," the record of the beginnings of the nations of antiquity. Professor W.F. Albright referred to it as "astonishingly accurate--it stands absolutely alone in ancient literature, without a remote parallel even among the Greeks" (*Recent Discoveries in Bible Lands*, pp. 70ff.).

Genesis chapter 11 tells of the Tower of Babel, the confusion of tongues, the dispersal of peoples, and the movement of Abraham and his family from Ur to Haran. King Ur-Nammu of Ur (2044 to 2007 B.C.) was supposedly commanded by the gods to build such a ziggurat, but a recovered tablet says it greatly offended the gods, so they threw it down in a night, confounded man's language, and spread people far and wide.

Worldwide "universals of language" suggest an original unity. Whatever method God used to "spread" people, this happening could explain "cavemen" (some people found themselves in lush areas, but others in more difficult areas, etc.). This demonstrated *devolution*, not *evolution.*

Ur and Haran were both cities of moon worship, connected by trade routes. Joshua 24:14 is relevant in regard to worship by the ancestors of Abraham at Ur. As Ur and Haran were in different countries (Gen. 11:31; Acts 7:4), the Ur of the Ebla tablets is a different center--in those tablets Haran is nearby. As with modern usage, similar names were at times used in different countries.

Genesis chapters 1 through 11 are at times "supra-historical," beyond present historical happenings, but they record actual happenings. They are a necessary introduction to Abraham, the father of the Hebrew people, uniquely tracing their ancestry to one man. We saw that these chapters are also the "seedplot of the Bible," as they introduce us to great doctrines about God Who is Creator, Revealer, Friend, Judge, Redeemer, Covenant-Keeper, and Sustainer. These doctrines are developed in later scriptures, but they are never put aside. The seed is often in the Old Testament, with the developed fruit in the New Testament.

The Genesis Approach to History

It is also important to recognize a certain aspect of the form of history recording in Genesis. Thus at Genesis 1:1 we read, *"In the beginning God created the heaven and the earth."* That is an all-inclusive statement, and what follows is a detailed elaboration of that first statement. It sets a pattern for other aspects of the history recording in Genesis. We have the whole account of creation given in some detail in Genesis chapter 1, with the heaven, the earth, the grass, the trees, the sun, the moon, the fish, the animals, and man all brought into being.

However, the Bible is not meant to be a geological

textbook in the modern sense, nor is it book about astronomy, zoology, or any of the other sciences that modern scholars continue to study. It is a record about man, and so in the first chapter of Genesis sufficient information is given to show the setting into which man was originally brought. Then all those other disciplines, those other areas of science and so much more, are put to one side and they are dealt with only for specific teaching purposes or as they are related in some way to the man whom God created.

When we come into the second chapter we are now given the details of the creation of man. It has been made quite clear in chapter 1, especially in verse 27, that God created both man and woman at that time of original creation. Now in chapter 2 the details are given, elaborating how first man and then the woman Eve were brought into being. This is not simply a second story of creation--a duplication or ''doublet'' as some critics have claimed. It is in fact the manner of history recording that we have in Genesis. We saw that the whole of creation is outlined in the first verse of Genesis, and the details are sufficiently elaborated for man's knowledge in the rest of Genesis chapter 1. Now in chapter 2 we have the elaboration of the preliminary statement which was made in chapter 1. Genesis chapter 1 gives the total picture; chapter 2 fills in the details of the major area to be dealt with (mankind).

This same principle is seen as we go on through Genesis. The early chapters of Genesis, right through from Genesis chapters 1 through 11, are a necessary introduction to the great man Abraham to whom we are now introduced. The Bible is not a history of all the nations of the world, and from the time of Abraham onward those other nations are dismissed except for their relevance in the history of Abraham and his descendants, and ultimately of the Lord Jesus Christ who was Himself, humanly speaking, a descendant from Abraham.

So in Genesis chapter 12 there is a new start made as the great man Abraham sets out to be a pilgrim, but as one who is journeying in the very presence of God. Clearly one of the purposes of Genesis chapters 1 through 11 were to give a necessary background to Abraham--including creation and the pre-flood world.

A Historical Principle with Ishmael ... and Esau

This same principle is again seen with the records about Ishmael. In Genesis 25:12 and the following verses we read details about the generations of Ishmael, but then at verse 19 the record comes back to Isaac. Several generations of Ishmael's descendants have been given, but from that point they are virtually dismissed. For the rest of Scripture they will be relevant only where their history touches that of the descendants of Abraham through Isaac.

The principle is again seen in the records about Esau. Jacob and Esau were both the sons of Isaac, but the record focuses on Jacob, even though Esau was originally the first-born. Jacob was to have the blessings of the firstborn, and so in Genesis 36:19 and the following verses we have the record of the sons of Esau. That record continues on to the end of the chapter in verse 43, and then in chapter 37 we return to Jacob. In verse 2 of that chapter we read, *"These are the generations of Jacob...."*

Once again we have seen that the one who is not in the direct line of descent toward the Messiah is put to one side and the record focuses on the direct line through Abraham to Christ.

This is an important fact to notice, for it explains some of the so-called problems of history recording in Genesis. It explains why there are two separate records of creation. It explains why the Table of the Nations is given in Genesis chapter 10. It explains how there is a narrowing-down process, with both Ishmael and Esau put to one side as the record zeroes in on the ones who will be the forefathers of the Lord Jesus Christ, the promised Messiah.

It is interesting to notice that the book of Matthew, the first book of the New Testament, commences with the genealogy of the Lord Jesus Christ. The zeroing-in process has its ultimate purpose shown in the revelation of the Lord Jesus Christ, the One who is there presented by Matthew as the Son of David, the Son of Abraham, and immediately it lists those through whom our Lord came.

This is a very interesting and relevant continuation of the process that is seen right there in Genesis chapter 1. The inner consistency and harmony of all Scripture is simply remarkable, and it is good to find some of the Divinely-given clues as we come to recognize that the Bible is the most accurate historical textbook the world has ever seen. And that history begins at Genesis chapter 1. The early chapters of Genesis are indeed the ''seedplot of the Bible''--both for doctrine and for history.

We are not surprised to find this inner harmony and consistency, for the world's greatest Teacher, the Son of God Himself, once declared, *''Thy word is truth''* (John 17:17).

A Bird's Eye View of the Seedplot ... and a Practical Application

We have seen that Genesis chapters 1 to 11 are the ''seedplot of the Bible.'' God is seen as :

Creator; Revealer; Friend; Judge; Redeemer; Restorer; Covenant-Keeper; and Sustainer.

Each of these points to Christ, and they have direct relevance for the Christian life of the believer today. We are a new creation with divine truth revealed to us by the indwelling

Holy Spirit of God. He makes it possible for us to be God's friends. Then, too, the One who judges our sin is also our Redeemer, the One who ''restored what He took not away.'' He restores to us the privilege of paradise and more. He sealed the new covenant with us in His own blood. And He sustains us in our daily walk with our risen Lord.

The stones continue to cry out as to the integrity of the Bible, God's Word of Truth.